GOD'S DOWNWARD MOBILITY

Sermons For Advent, Christmas
And Epiphany, Cycle B
Gospel Texts

John A. Stroman

CSS Publishing Company, Inc., Lima, Ohio

GOD'S DOWNWARD MOBILITY

Copyright © 1996 by
CSS Publishing Company, Inc.
Lima, Ohio

All rights reserved. No part of this publication may be reproduced in any manner whatsoever without the prior permission of the publisher, except in the case of brief quotations embodied in critical articles and reviews. Inquiries should be addressed to: Permissions, CSS Publishing Company, Inc., P.O. Box 4503, Lima, Ohio 45802-4503.

Scripture quotations are from the *New Revised Standard Version of the Bible*, copyright 1989 by the Division of Christian Education of the National Council of the Churches of Christ in the USA. Used by permission.

Library of Congress Cataloging-in-Publication Data

Stroman, John A.
   God's downward mobility : sermons for Advent, Christmas, and Epiphany : Cycle B, Gospel texts / John A. Stroman.
      p.   cm.
   ISBN 0-7880-0789-0 (pbk.)
   1. Advent sermons. 2. Christmas sermons. 3. Epiphany season — Sermons. 4. Sermons, American. 5. Bible. N.T. Gospels—Sermons. I. Title.
BV4254.5.S77   1996
252'.61—dc20   96-11281
                                                                              CIP

*To the congregation at Pasadena Community Church
whose prayers and support have made
all of this possible.*

Table Of Contents

Introduction	7
Advent 1	11
Ready Or Not He Comes	
Mark 13:24-37 (C)	
Mark 13:33-37 (RC)	
Advent 2	17
Have You Heard The Good News?	
Mark 1:1-8	
Advent 3	23
A Voice Crying In The Wilderness	
John 1:6-8, 19-28	
Advent 4	29
How Odd Of God	
Luke 1:26-38	
Christmas Eve/Day	35
The Highest In The Lowest	
Luke 2:1-20 (C)	
Luke 2:15-20 (RC)	
Christmas 1	41
Discovering The Unexpected	
Luke 2:22-40	
Christmas 2	47
God Is Down To Earth	
John 1:1-18	
Epiphany 1	53
(Baptism Of The Lord)	
A Moment Of Decision	
Mark 1:4-11 (C)	
Mark 1:7-11 (RC)	

Epiphany 2   59
Ordinary Time 2
   Pass It On
   John 1:43-51 (C)
   John 1:35-43 (RC)

Epiphany 3   65
Ordinary Time 3
   Drop-Everything-Discipleship
   Mark 1:14-20

Epiphany 4   71
Ordinary Time 4
   By What Authority?
   Mark 1:21-28

Epiphany 5   77
Ordinary Time 5
   The Demanding Crowd
   Mark 1:29-39

Epiphany 6   83
Ordinary Time 6
   A Hands-On Religion
   Mark 1:40-45

Epiphany 7   89
Ordinary Time 7
   The Power Of A Rumor
   Mark 2:1-12

Epiphany 8   93
Ordinary Time 8
   What Shall We Do With The New Wine?
   Mark 2:13-22

The Transfiguration Of The Lord   99
(Last Sunday After The Epiphany)
   With Our Heads In The Clouds
   Mark 9:2-9

C — Revised Common Lectionary; RC — Roman Catholic Lectionary

Introduction

The preacher has a great opportunity for proclamation beginning with the Advent texts. I find this one of the most uplifting and inspiring seasons of the Christian year. The music for Advent and Christmas is spectacular and the biblical texts are extremely hopeful. I am convinced that the message revealed in the biblical texts of Advent and Christmas have their roots in the Old Testament. The biblical message of liberation and freedom began in the exodus from Egypt and it reaches its fullest expression of deliverance in the Advent of Jesus Christ at Bethlehem. From Exodus to Advent, from Egypt to Bethlehem is one continuous theme of a loving God whose main desire is to set the captive free.

There is a biblical framework here that the preacher needs to keep in mind. God chose Israel not because it was a great nation but because it was the "least of all peoples," a tiny, insignificant nation, the doormat of the ancient world on which the great empires wiped their feet. When weak Israel was pitted against Egypt, God did not side with Pharaoh, the powerful political leader, but with the oppressed menial servants, the scum of society, the slaves.

This same theme is evident in the Advent when Mary sings the Magnificat, her song of praise to God:

> *He has shown strength with his arm, he has scattered the proud in the imagination of their hearts, he has put down the mighty from their thrones, and exalted those of low degree; he has filled the hungry with good things, and the rich he has sent away.*
> — Luke 1:51-53

When Jesus preaches in Nazareth, he takes his cue from Isaiah:

The Spirit of the Lord is upon me, because he has anointed me to preach good news to the poor. He has sent me to proclaim release to the captives and recovering the sight of the blind, and to set at liberty those who are oppressed, and to proclaim the acceptable year of the Lord.
— Luke 4:18-19

Is not the liberation of oppressed people from the biblical narrative the possibility of liberation for all oppressed people today? As Robert McAfee Brown reminds us, if God took sides back then, it is clear that God continues to take sides today, identifying with the oppressed and challenging their oppressors. *And this means that all who claim to believe in God and seek to do God's will must take sides.*

When God chooses sides, God brings hope to a previously hopeless situation. At the Exodus, Miriam sang and beat on the drums: "Let us sing unto the Lord, for he has done a noble deed; horse and rider he has thrown into the sea" (Exodus 15:20-21). Thus sang Hannah, "The bows of the mighty are broke, but the feeble gird on strength" (1 Samuel 2:4). Prior to the Advent of Jesus, Mary's song of praise is also a song of great hope: "He has put down the mighty from their thrones, and exalted those of low degree" (Luke 1:52).

The Bible reveals a God of surprise. He calls his creation into life out of waste, wilderness and darkness. He liberates a tiny colony enslaved by a powerful nation and casts the chariots of the powerful into the sea. He led Jesus, damned by the law and crucified by Roman power, out of death into new life. With Christ God shows his love for all persons. What started as freedom for a small nomadic tribe is now freedom for all. God's nobility should reflect itself in everyone. In Christ, God lifts the degraded and insulted, the oppressed and burdened to his grace. Thus, the final word in the liberation of God is joy. Joy to the world, the Lord is come!

This expresses my biblical and theological presuppositions as I approach these Advent-Christmas-Epiphany texts. I have shared these words in one way or another with the congregation at Pasadena Community Church, where I have served as their pastor for the last eight years. I appreciate their thoughtful comments and critiques and I am pleased to share these sermons with you.

I have used for this series the title *God's Downward Mobility*. Today, we hear a lot about "upward mobility" through wealth, affluence, power, and position. The overwhelming desire and passion of our contemporary culture is to achieve "upward mobility." The birth of Jesus is God's "downward mobility." In him the word became flesh. God in Christ comes down to our world to the level of our hurts and needs. Paul expressed it accurately: "In Christ, God was reconciling the world to himself" (2 Corinthians 5:17). What better way to describe this than "God's Downward Mobility"?

> John A. Stroman
> Pasadena Community Church
> St. Petersburg, Florida

Mark 13:24-17 (C)
Mark 13:33-37 (RC)

Advent 1

Ready Or Not — He Comes

And what I say to you I say to all — Keep awake!
—Mark 13:37

There is a passage in the old Jewish book of *Zohar*, that goes like this: "Whenever the Jews on earth rejoice in their festivals, they give praise to the Lord. They put on fine clothes and pile their tables with good food. So the angel asks, 'Why do the Jews pamper themselves so much?' And God answers, 'They have a distinguished guest today. I am with them.'" Today is a very special day. We are preparing for a very special guest. It is the first Sunday of Advent. Our celebration begins with the word "Emmanuel," which means, "God is with us."

Have you noticed every time God seeks to change the world God allows a baby to be born? First, it was an infant in the bulrushes of Egypt and then a child in a manger in Bethlehem. God always comes to us in the most unexpected manner. God's self-disclosure through the biblical narrative is usually in a quiet and low-key, almost unseen, way. It catches us by surprise because we don't expect it to be that way. The advent of Jesus' birth is no exception. The good news today is that "God is coming." Take heed. Whether it be heard as good news or bad news depends, to a great extent, on your location or where you happen to be and under what circumstances you find yourself when you hear it. Today's message, good or bad, is that God is coming. Keep awake!

Today's text has a strong eschatological imagery. It talks about the sun and the moon darkened, the stars falling, and powers shaking. It sounds like a text for the second coming of Christ rather than his birth.

This is not what you would expect for the first Sunday of Advent. There must be some mistake. This passage is more appropriate for Lent than Advent. We are ready for the Annunciation not the Apocalypse. We should be on our way to Bethlehem not Jerusalem. We are four weeks away from Jesus' birth, and this passage is two days away from Jesus' death. We are ready to buy gifts and to prepare for the baby's birth, but Mark will not let us.

Mark 13, Luke 21, and Matthew 24 are part of what is called the "little Apocalypse." It is the happy hunting ground for those fascinated by the end of time. All three borrow from Daniel's "abomination of desolation" for their apocalyptic imagery. Mark 13 figures prominently in books by doomsdayers and by preachers who are more interested in the next world than this one.

Why is Mark 13 used for this first Sunday of Advent? Because the message in this text has a good word for us during Advent. Notice that Mark stresses "staying awake," "be on your guard," "be alert," and, three times in the chapter, "keep awake." If not, you will miss the whole thing. Many have. Many will again.

Advent is an awesome experience of God getting in touch with human beings. So much of it seems too good to be true. It is awesome in the sense that God is veiled in human flesh and "in Christ God was reconciling the world to himself" (2 Corinthians 5:19). Mind-boggling to think that Jesus Christ became, in the words of the apostle Paul, the "visible likeness of the invisible God."

This text in Mark 13 reminds us today that Advent is upon us. We need to get our lives in order or we will miss the whole thing again.

Advent Is An Opportunity To Regain A Sense Of Wonder

Dag Hammarskjold said, "God does not die on the day we cease to believe in him, but we die on the day our lives cease to be illumined by the steady radiance of God's love." It is at that point that wonder leaves our lives.

When was the last time you really got excited about something? How long has it been since you got a lump in your throat or shivers up your spine? We seem to have become so dead to feeling, so void of wonder. Television, radio, sonic booms, traffic congestion, saturation advertising, and media exposure to world calamities have killed off our senses. We have become numb to feeling. We do not even realize that wonder has disappeared from our existence. We have lost touch with the world around us. We live in a day of "high tech" and "low touch."

We have developed what has been called the CNN Complex. This syndrome was first identified during the Gulf War. People around the world were glued to their television sets because of CNN. They watched the live battle scenes of the Gulf War and the ballistic attacks over Baghdad day after day along with the Scud missile attacks on Israel. The same thing took place on a worldwide scope with the O.J. Simpson murder trial.

This coverage has created post-modern addicts who are addicted to news and bulletins. We seem to have become pathologically addicted simply to information itself. We crave information for information's sake, without comprehending it. This has made it possible for the computer to open to us the Information Superhighway. The CNN Complex seems to have created a world without feeling and mystery, deadening our sense of wonder.

But Advent presents us with the opportunity to regain our sense of wonder. It interjects into our bloodstream not only wonder, but mystery and expectation. Advent reminds us that something exciting is about to happen. Howard Thurman states in his poem that Advent is a time for the singing of angels.

> *There must be always remaining*
> *in everyone's life*
> *some place for the singing of angels —*

some place for that which in itself is breathlessly beautiful . . .

Despite all the crassness of life,
Despite all the hardness of life,
Despite all the harsh discords of life,
Life is saved by the singing of angels.[1]

During Advent we experience the reality of God's grace that is beyond explanation and reason. It has about it a mystery. But this is always true of grace. For the grace of God in Jesus Christ is not only surprising but amazing.

Advent Reveals The Beauty And Grandeur Of God

Virginia Owens in her book, *And The Trees Clap Their Hands*, suggests that we lose the wonder of it all, because along the way everything becomes "merely." Things are "merely" stars, sunset, rain, flowers, and mountains. Their connection with God's creation is lost. During this Advent season many things are just "merely." It becomes "merely" Bethlehem, a stable, a birth — we have no feeling of wonder or mystery. That is what familiarity can do to us over the years.

Owens goes on to say that it is this "merely" quality of things that leads to crime. It is "merely" a thing — I'll take it. It is "merely" an object — I'll destroy it. It is this "merely" quality of things and life that leads to war. We shall lose "merely" a few thousand men, but it will be worth it.

Within the Advent narrative nothing is "merely." Things are not "merely" things, but are part of God's grand design. Common things, such as motherhood, a birth, a child, now have new meaning. This is not "merely" the world, but a world that is charged with the beauty and grandeur of God's design. It is a world so loved by God that God gave his only Son. What is so great about the Advent season is that everything appears charged with the beauty and grandeur of God.

There Is The Feeling That Something Great Is About To Happen

During Advent we walk on tip-toe with hushed voices, because we have the feeling that something great is about to happen. Listen again to the familiar story of Bethlehem. Do not allow its familiarity to put a glaze over your eyes or deaden your sense of wonder. It is a story that will be read in every part of the world this Advent season, in every dialect and in every language. It will be dramatized in pageants, cantatas and concerts. Many will consider it interesting, pretty, amusing, and entertaining, like a fairy tale. Some will list it along with other holiday fantasies such as *Lion King* and *Swan Princess*.

It has become wrapped up in so much sentimental embroidery that its stark realism is lost. Its characters have acquired "halos," becoming something quite out of this world. Take a closer look at this story and you will notice the characters are not people with halos, but ordinary men and women of flesh and blood, fears and frustrations, anxiety and hope, just like us.

Mary and Joseph are not stained-glass saints. They are ordinary artisans of humble faith with a sincere commitment to do the will of God. The child is not an infant prodigy of Raphael's *Madonna,* but a kicking, crying, helpless baby in Mary's arms, who will grow up in a world that will never really understand him.

The shepherds are not idyllic figures, but rough and tough, unkempt men of the Judean plains. They are the migrant workers of the first century. They are huddled together for warmth on the hillside on a bleak winter's night when they are visited by the heavenly host. In the birth of Jesus, who was born within a working class family amid the poverty of the Judean hills, we find ourselves face to face with God.

On this first Sunday of Advent there is a new sense of hope, optimism, joy, and love being unleashed upon us. There is a feeling of great expectation that something significant is about to happen as we sing together that great hymn of Advent, "O come, O come, Emmanuel and ransom captive Israel."

Just as Advent moves us toward the remembrance of the birth of Jesus in Bethlehem in the first century, it also reminds us that most of the world was preoccupied and utterly unprepared for that first Advent and many missed the whole thing. The basic question that is prompted by our text is: "Will we miss the whole thing again?"

Our text urges us to keep vigilant. Keep alert! Watch! Ready or not — Christ is coming!

---

1. Howard Thurman, *The Mood Of Christmas* (Harper and Rowe, 1973), p. 41.

Mark 1:1-8   Advent 2

Have You Heard The Good News?

The beginning of the good news of Jesus Christ, the Son of God.   — Mark 1:1

Have you heard the good news? Mark starts off his gospel with the announcement of the coming of the good news. He reveals to us the content and the nature of that good news. It is "the good news of Jesus Christ, the Son of God."

That is what the Advent is all about — the preparation for the coming of Jesus Christ. This good news is centered in Jesus Christ. This is the mood and feeling that is captured by the African-American spiritual:

> *Go tell it on the mountain,*
>   *over the hills and everywhere;*
> *Go tell it on the mountain,*
>   *that Jesus Christ is born.*

The good news is that Jesus was born in an obscure village in an out-of-the-way place that was shadowy, barren and unknown. Today, Christ comes to the shadowy and barren places of our lives. This is what Advent is all about. This is the good news!

Jesus was born amid the poverty and obscurity of those Judean hills, but the fact remains that he transformed human life in the first century. It all began in such lowliness and unpretentiousness. Today Christ comes to those shadowy and barren places of our lives and brings the light of God's love and grace. It was good news for the first century and it is good news for our century. This is the hope and joy of the Advent message. This is the good news! In Bethlehem heaven touched the earth as never before. Today, the good news of the gospel touches our hearts and lives with the announcement that God is with us. Jesus walked along the shores of Galilee, but the good news is that today he walks our city streets. He is with us amid life's strains and stresses.

God Is Personal And Close

Look at the humble setting where this message of good news first appeared. It did not appear to have a ghost of a chance of surviving. The birth of Jesus took place in a tiny country. Palestine is only about 150 miles from north to south. It is about the size of the state of New Hampshire. How could the good news that came to that community ever become good news for all the world today? Jesus was born into a Jewish family. Palestine was inhabited by Jews, but the Jews deliberately isolated themselves from other cultures and other communities. How could good news that came to a country which had a deliberate policy of isolation be good news for all the world? The good news first appeared to the Jews, but at the time the Jews were under Roman occupation. During their entire history they rarely knew what freedom and independence were. How could this good news that came to those who were so isolated and occupied by a foreign power ever be good news for all the world? The answer is simple. The message of the good news of Jesus Christ is one that is about personal relationships. It is about the relationship between women, men, and God. Personal relationships don't change. Love, hate, honor, and loyalty remain the same. Jesus came to meet the basic human needs of the first century and our century. Jesus entered into life "then and there," and "here and now."

Jesus met the needs of the first century world, and the good news is he meets the needs of those in today's world. As Walter

Wink reminds us in his powerful book, *Engaging the Powers,* "Jesus identifies today with every victim of torture, incest, or rape; with every peasant caught in the crossfire of an enemy patrol; with every single one of the forty thousand children who die each day of hunger …with the Alzheimer's patient who is slowly losing the capacity of recognition and the AIDS patient who is barely holding on to life" (p. 142). The good news is that in Jesus God became flesh and knows life exactly as we know it, every pain, every tear, every aspect. Emmanuel, truly God is with us. That is the good news.

God Of Compassion And Concern

The message of the good news of Jesus was earthshaking for the first century world. They had never heard such a teaching about God. For the first century Greek mind, the idea of God was one of absolute serenity, which nothing in heaven or earth could affect. They saw life in terms of a God who was serene, isolated, untouchable and freed from all feeling and emotion. For the Stoics, God was by nature incapable of feeling. In the first century world, the idea of God was one of detachment and indifference to human need.

The difference that good news in Jesus Christ made to the people of the first century was to reveal a God who cares desperately, a God who is involved in human situations. Against the backdrop of this first century world that considered all the deities as being insulated from human need and emotionless to human concern comes the good news of Jesus Christ. Barbara Taylor Brown reminds us that "when you look at him (Jesus), you see God. When you listen to him, you hear God. Not because he has taken God's place, but because he is the clear window God has glazed into flesh and blood — the porthole between this world and the next, the passageway between heaven and earth" (*The Preaching Life*). That was good news for the first century world and that is good news for our world.

Never before had God been defined in such loving, kind, gracious, and caring terms. This was unthinkable for the first century world to whom Mark was writing his gospel. It seemed incomprehensible to those of Mark's day that the Son of God would be born of a woman in the tiny village of Bethlehem in a stable cave on a cold winter's night. But the apostle stated this event in terms that are true for all ages when he declared "that . . . in Christ God was reconciling the world to himself" (2 Corinthians 5:19).

Surprised By Grace

The primary expression of this good news is grace. God through grace has taken the initiative to bring this world back to God. In the birth of Jesus a relationship between God and humankind has been made possible. It can never be earned, since it is a result of grace; it can only be received. In fact, grace cannot really be described as it can be experienced. It is more "caught" than "taught." It is defined in the scriptures as "steadfast love." Therefore, as "steadfast love," it is reliable and constant and trustworthy — the very thing that is needed in our lives today.

Grace has been defined as love in action. That is a good definition of the grace of God. It is love in action — love in human action. The Bible clearly points out that God's relationship with men and women is not based on the fact that we offer something to God, but on the fact that God offers everything to us. God offers love to us not because we are good or great, but simply because God is love. That is the kind of God God is.

The Advent is the supreme example of grace. The incarnation focuses in on a single point, a moment in history, on what God through grace has been doing always and everywhere. The incarnation becomes the essential clue to the interpretation of the whole mission of God to the world.

What surprises us about God's grace in regard to the Advent is the notion that God should take on flesh and dwell among us. What a surprise that the Son of God was born into a lower-class Jewish family living on the fringe of poverty and obscurity and was permitted to die in disgrace as a common criminal! That is the surprising way that God, through grace, chose to do it.

The fact is we are always surprised by grace. Because it is God's grace, it comes to us on God's terms. Grace is the unmerited, unearned, undeserved goodness of God that is showered upon our lives. In the Old Testament, God loves and chooses Israel to reveal

God's purpose and will. Not because Israel is good or great. God does not need Israel or depend on her. Yet God loves Israel. Why? Because it is God's nature to love. What can be said of Israel can be said of us. Why does God love us? Simply because God is love. There is no other reason to explain why God should take the risk. This is the surprising nature of God's grace.

God's Love Is Persistent

Mark opens his gospel with the declaration: "the good news of the gospel of Jesus Christ." Here we discover God's love in action in the life of Jesus. The whole Bible is a commentary on the grace of God which seeks to save. Why wasn't Israel given up as hopeless because of her constant bickering, criticism, and failure? Why wasn't Jacob cast out on the scrap heap for his warped and twisted ways? Why wasn't David disowned by God for the dark and degrading deed that made his name a byword in the land? Why wasn't Peter left to sink after his base denial? Why wasn't Saul of Tarsus, persecutor, blasphemer, hater of Christ, blotted out of the Book of Life forever? Why is it that God has not given up on us? We have spurned God's love, polluted God's creation, and mocked God's purpose with cruel acts of inhumanity. Why doesn't God just go ahead and allow us to self-destruct? Because there is nothing in heaven or on earth so dogged, determined, stubborn, and persistent as the grace of God that wills to save.

Tom Long asks the question in his book *Shepherds and Bathrobes*: "Have you ever noticed where God placed his treasure that he was seeking to deposit on the earth?" The treasure is not gold, but gospel. Not silver, but good news. Not hard, cold cash, but grace, love, and peace.

He points out that God could have left it with the politicians, those who are responsible for collecting taxes, building schools, and passing laws, but God didn't. God could have left this treasure with Zechariah, the high priest, but his unbelief took him out of the picture. Long states that God left the treasure in the least likely of places: in the love, care, and nurture of a first century peasant woman chosen as the "handmaiden of the Lord." God's treasure was left with the most powerless figure in the ancient world. Doesn't that tell you something about God's grace in today's world?

We are constantly surprised by grace. Grace may be surprising, but grace is always amazing. God comes to us in the most unlikely place — Bethlehem. God comes through the most unlikely of people — Mary. God comes to us under the most unlikely circumstances — the poverty of the Judean hills. Today, God through Christ comes again to the most unlikely people — you and me. God comes to us at the level of our need. Knowing that we cannot go where God is, God comes to us where we are. This is what Mark calls "the good news of the gospel of Jesus Christ."

John 1:6-8, 19-28   Advent 3

A Voice Crying In The Wilderness

I am the voice of one crying in the wilderness . . . .
— John 1:23

The people wondered who John the Baptist was. He appeared as a rather strange person who came from the wilderness, preaching repentance, dressed in camel's hair, surviving on a diet of locust and wild honey. John the Baptist was the beginning of the good news of Jesus Christ. Yet his message of good news seemed as strange as his attire. It was good news involving repentance, and repentance involved change. That is good news to some people but it is bad news to others. It was good news for the oppressed. It was bad news for the oppressors. It was good news for those who suffered pain. It was bad news for those who inflicted pain. It was good news for the masses in John's day who were waiting to hear that things can change. It was bad news for those who wanted to maintain life as usual. The gospel of Jesus Christ begins with the arrival of John the Baptist, who proclaims the coming of one who will ransom captive Israel. He is the forerunner of the good news, the news of change, of a new beginning and a fresh start. John declares one is coming "who is more powerful than I."

The Wilderness Experience

As Leonard Sweet points out, the *wilderness theme* is extremely important in understanding this text and John's place in this new exodus. Just as the first Exodus took place in the wilderness this second mighty act of God's self-disclosure also takes place in the wilderness. Let us consider the wilderness, not as a place of testing and judgment, but rather as a place that can cleanse, purge, and renew.

The crowd asked John, "Who are you?" John confessed that he was not the Christ. They asked, "What then, are you Elijah?" He answered, "I am not." "Are you the prophet?" meaning Jeremiah. "No," John replied. "Then who are you?" the crowd demanded. John's response was, "I am the voice of one crying in the wilderness." He was clear to point out that he was not the Messiah, but rather he was only a voice, telling them to get ready for the Messiah is coming. John told them that he was nobody, but the one who is coming is somebody. John was saying, "I am the pointer, the preparer of the way, the forerunner. You need to look to the one who is coming after me. He is preferred before me. I am not even worthy to untie the thong of his sandal. Look to him!"

John Prepares The Way

Martin Luther in his exposition of John 1 points out that Jesus came in simplicity, not ostentatiously, to win the world through his life and his teachings rather than with a sword and coercion. Therefore, God sent to prepare the way for Jesus not an angel, but a man. A man who came not of his own accord but, as the text tells us, "a man who was sent by God, whose name was John."

John the Baptist was a prophet. Although the prophet's message is relevant, truthful, and urgent, it is one that the people do not easily receive. We are not particularly fond of those people who tell us what is wrong with us. The prophet's frankness, boldness, and honesty are more than the people can bear to hear. Both John's attire and his preaching of repentance embody a wilderness motif. Today, we ignore the prophets, considering them as strange people. Strange in the sense that they can't accept the *status-quo* like the rest of the people. Strange in that they are not willing to overlook inconsistencies and injustices as most people are willing to do. Strange in the sense that they seem overly conscientious with a keen sense of compassion and concern. There is a tendency to ignore the prophets because they make us feel uncomfortable, and by ignoring them, we hope they will go away. At times, we have taken more drastic measures, by stoning the prophets, in hopes of silencing their voices. After the deaths of Martin Luther King, Jr., and Robert Kennedy, the folk singers sang the ballad which asked, "Where have all of the prophets gone?"

The Voice Of The Prophet

We try, but we cannot silence the voice of the prophet. When one is struck down, God raises up another. Martin Luther King's voice was silenced, but Bishop Desmond Tutu's voice became strident. Today the prophet's voice is still crying out about brutality, violence, and the lack of moral integrity. We are witnessing the disintegration of society as the prophets have warned, with the breakdown of the home, the violence in the streets, and the eroding of human values by the drug culture, resulting in human life cracking and breaking under the stress and strain of it all. The modern prophets are telling us that we must deal with drugs, violence, racism, and crime, or we will not survive as a nation or as a people. Our imagined fears and conspiracies became realities with the bombing of the federal building in Oklahoma City.

There are other prophetic voices in our midst who are telling us that we cannot disregard creation, nature, or the environment, for to do so is to destroy human life itself. Several years ago Rachel Carson wrote *Silent Spring*. She told us that if we continued to use pesticides and insecticides, especially DDT, that we would wake up some day to a silent spring. The birds would no longer sing, because there would be no birds. Eventually there would be no life, period. She was mocked and ridiculed. After these many years she is now held in high esteem and appreciated. Studies have now shown how devastating DDT has been on human and animal life. The world is grateful to her that DDT was finally banned before it could spread further havoc on our planet. Many people today are still suffering from the lingering effects of DDT.

Crying In The Wilderness

The prophet is the voice of one "crying in the wilderness." Because of the truthfulness of the prophet's message, which for the most part is disturbing and upsetting, we have forced him into the wilderness. But we know that many of the prophetic voices which God has raised up in our day are right. They are telling us that if we ignore the homeless, the powerless, and the marginal of our day, we do so at our own peril. They are right. But we do not want to be reminded of our moral responsibilities, failures, and short-comings. We do not want to be reminded that we are responsible for the consequences of our behavior. Therefore, the prophet is crying in the "wilderness" because we have abandoned him to the wilderness. We have "ears to hear," yet we do not hear. We have "eyes to see," but we do not see. We have chosen not to hear or see.

Jesus Identifies With Human Need

There is a unique relationship between Jesus and John the Baptist. This is seen in the close association of their mothers prior to their births and in John's preparation for the inauguration of Jesus' ministry. But most importantly it is in Jesus' baptism by John. Why was Jesus baptized by John? There seems to be only one reason. It was not because Jesus needed to repent of his sins, but rather because Jesus wanted to identify with both John's message and the people. The only way for Jesus to minister to the masses and reveal his love for them was to enter the water and be baptized with them. Jesus felt the need to stand with them on their level. He got down in the water with John and the people. Jesus' identifying with masses of people at the level of their need is the good news of the gospel.

The good news of the gospel is that Jesus meets us at the level of our need. Think of this good news in regard to the person who is living on a $100 a year. He has no car. His home is the size of a backyard toolshed. He has no television, radio, or appliances, and is without the benefit of running water or electricity. He represents over half of the people of the world. For such people the words of Jesus are good news indeed.

The good news comes to the brokenhearted, the lonely, and the forgotten. Talk to administrators of nursing homes and let them tell you about how some of their residents have been abandoned. No one ever comes to see them. The nursing home staff is their entire family. What an important role care givers provide in today's society. What about those partners in marriage who best describe their relationship as a "cold war"? Feeling, love, and emotion have evaporated, leaving merely a skeleton of an existence. What about that sobbing suicidal teenager who is making that last desperate call on a telephone hotline to a counseling center? The message of Advent is one of hope. Hope, because it reminds us that we are not alone. We have not been left to the mercy of devastating circumstances. The word is *Emmanuel*, God is with us.

Jesus Comes To Put Our Lives Together

What do these words of the advent of Jesus Christ mean to the broken, forsaken, and shattered lives among us? It means that Christ has come with a glue pot to pick up the broken pieces and make life whole again. The message of Advent is that Jesus comes with a radiance and joy that penetrates such despair and heavy heartedness.

Think of those among us whose spirit has grown faint. The couple who is worried about how they are going to pay the medical expenses of a desperately sick child. That father who faces the new year with the possibility he will be unemployed. The older couple who has been informed that their son and his family are moving in with them because their son has lost his job. The single parent mother who can barely drag herself out of bed in the morning because she feels so burnt-out and so used-up. The older man who sees the younger generation undoing all the reforms it took a lifetime to achieve. The elderly woman who asks of her pastor when he comes to visit her to pray for the Lord to take her. What does the coming of Jesus mean for them? For us?

Listen to the words of the Old Testament lesson for today coming from Isaiah 40 as the prophet proclaims,

Comfort, O comfort my people, says your God. (v. 1)
He gives power to the faint, and strengthens the powerless. (v. 29)
But those who wait for the Lord shall renew their strength .... (v. 31a)

What Isaiah prophesied Jesus came to fulfill. Amid all of our human brokenness Jesus brings to us the comfort of his healing presence. If you want to see the stars on a December night you must get away from the light of the city. You need to get out into the countryside, away from all the artificial light, to where it is very dark. There you will be able to see the fragile light of the stars. It is fragile because there are so many things, such as smog, pollution, and artificial light that can obscure and hide the stars' beauty. That light that comes into the world in Jesus is so fragile that we must get away from the humdrum, the shopping crowds, the lights and the tinsel, and the daily course of things to observe its meaning for us. We need to find that place this Advent where we can be silent, reflective, and prayerful, and wait for our eyes to behold the radiance of God's love for us in Jesus Christ. Do not allow anything this Christmas to obscure this message.

Luke 1:26-38 — Advent 4

How Odd Of God

"Greetings, favored one! The Lord is with you." But she was much perplexed by his words and pondered what sort of greeting this might be.
— Luke 1:28-29

In every generation if we are to apprehend the abiding forces that will dominate and direct the future, then we must believe in the minute, the diminutive, and the inconspicuous, as is seen in such New Testament words as "mustard seed" and "leaven." The most remembered events turn out to be not the vociferous and noisy affairs that split the eardrums of their contemporaries, but rather the embryonic, the secretive, and often the imperceptible. When the masses of West Germans danced on the Berlin Wall and thousands of East Germans passed through it, little did the world know that this was a result of a prayer service that had been held in Nikolai Church in downtown Leipzig. Eventually, this quiet, imperceptible group of people gathering for what the world considered a harmless time for prayer spilled out into the streets, forcing the opening of the Berlin Wall.

All Saving Ideas Are Born Small

Yes, all saving ideas are born small, often obscure and at times unnoticed. Like the birth of two babies, one among the bulrushes in Egypt and another in the stable-cave in Bethlehem. The manner that God has chosen to come into life always appears to be rather low key. God shuns the spectacular and uses the ordinary.

The Advent is no exception. What is more casual than the birth of a child? The babe in Bethlehem always appears to be less than he really is. Like a child born in poverty and obscurity. Like a young man growing up and being unnoticed for years while living with a carpenter's family in Nazareth. Like a prisoner refusing to answer the false accusations of a judge. Like a man riding on the back of a donkey, whose coming was so common and so ordinary that the masses overlooked him. How odd of God to be so casual and so down-to-earth.

God seldom acts in a manner we expect. God works through people and events that seem strange and unrelated to us, especially at Advent. It may appear odd to us that God would use the ordinary and the common, but if you know your Bible this would not surprise you. This is how God has always done it. Our problem is that we have seen too many Cecil B. de Mille's films with all the thunder and lighting and we have failed to read the text. Look closely at what is taking place in this birth narrative in the New Testament. Look at the locations, the time, and especially the people involved. Let me share with you a few observations.

God Chooses The Unexpected

How odd of God that God would reveal such an awesome message to such ordinary people. This message was not given to Herod in his palace in Jerusalem, nor to Caesar Augustus on his mighty throne in Rome, nor to the priests, rabbis, scribes or scholars, but to the shepherds keeping watch over their flocks by night. How odd that God would first declare that message to shepherds. There must have been some mix-up, some mistake. You would have thought this message would have first hit the UP wires along with the great dailies in Rome, Athens, Corinth, Alexandria, and Jerusalem. What went wrong with Gabriel's public relations? The great and important people in the world centers of power and politics did not receive advance notice. They never got the word. How odd of God! Is this any way to bring the Son of

God into the world? Is this any way to treat the birth of a king? But when you come right down to it, with everything we have come to know about Jesus' life, this appears to be the right place, at the right time, among the right people.

Who were these shepherds anyway? Let me tell you who they were. They were the migrant farm laborers of first century Palestine. They moved from one location to another seeking adequate grazing lands for their sheep. It was to these simple men of the field that God's message of the birth of Jesus first came to the earth. The highest announcement came to the lowest people.

Mary — Inconspicuous And Unexpected

How odd that God should choose Mary. As we come to think about the unexpected, the lowly and the inconspicuous person being the vessel of hope and change, certainly Mary comes to mind. There are things about Mary that really catch our attention. Hans Kung, the Roman Catholic theologian, reminds us that there are two features of Mary's image that are solidly rooted in the scriptures. First, she is human, a wife and a mother with all the earthiness that this may entail. Second, she is an example, a model of the Christian faith. Her faith felt both the sword of scandal, dissension, and contradiction. Notice the words of the text,

> *"Greetings, favored one! The Lord is with you." But she was much perplexed by his words and pondered what sort of greeting this might be.*
> — Luke 1:28-29

After Jesus' birth in Bethlehem Mary returned to Nazareth. These were long, hard years of survival in the back hill country of Judea. Mary's baby would grow into manhood in Nazareth and face a life of unending danger. He was loved by the common folks and despised by the political rulers. The religious leaders thought him a heretic and excommunicated him, and his nation thought him a traitor and crucified him. This was something that Mary could not quite figure out or understand.

Mary must have thought, "Is this what it means to be favored by God?" What a change from the starlit night in Bethlehem to the foot of the cross — from ecstasy to agony. Mary had discovered what many Christians have come to know, that to be called of God is to suffer with God. I wonder what Mary wanted her boy to be? A carpenter like his father, possibly. A rabbi? Maybe. Who knows? One thing is certain, she was not prepared for what he became.

There are many things in this birth narrative that seem strange, even odd to us, coming from our world of power politics and mega-institutions. But this is the manner that God has consistently chosen to come into the midst of life. A girl who is barely a teenager, of humble background, reared in the hill country of Judea, is chosen to be "the handmaiden of the Lord." I wonder if we can grasp the significance of this event. Mary was a woman, poor and young. The status of a woman in the first century was nothing. Yet, she was chosen to become the mother of God.

The Ordinary Became Extraordinary

Things appear odd to us because God does not follow our expectations. Instead of coming in the usual places, such as our homes and our churches, God may appear this Christmas on the streets of some city in Eastern Europe, or on a college campus, or in the scientist's lab. Before you decide that is nonsense, consider that it is not any more nonsensical than his birth in the first century in a stable cave.

We expect Jesus to come in the familiar, especially in the familiar carols. For some he may come that way, yet for others he may come in sounds so primitive it may not even resemble music. Or he may come in a place that we would consider unworthy of his coming. We expect him to come in the familiar language of the Bible, especially the language of our favorite translation. But it could be that he may come in some new language that is so vernacular that it may appear offensive. I would remind you that Jerome's translation of the scriptures in the fourth century from the Greek to the Latin was called the Vulgate, for that very same reason: people thought it to be a vulgar language. It was hard for them to accept anything as sacred and mysterious as Holy Writ to be so common and ordinary in its language.

The fact remains, God never acts in the manner we expect. God works through people and events that appear strange and unrelated to us. "God works in mysterious ways his wonders to perform." Who would have ever thought that the kingdom of peace would come through a child born to such humble parents? If God can use these humble vessels for God's eternal purpose, think what God can do with you. God uses the most ordinary people for the most extraordinary tasks.

Nobody Becomes Somebody

Several years ago I visited a man in a nursing home. Life was difficult for him and he constantly complained because he had no visitors and felt lonely and neglected. He seemed to have every right to complain as he did, considering the circumstances under which he lived. I went to see him just before Christmas. There were Christmas cards on his wall and a poinsettia plant on the table and he told me that the night before carolers from a local church came by and sang Christmas carols for him. I asked him how he was doing and he said, "At Christmas time I am somebody."

A nobody is a somebody at Christmas. All of the things that surround the birth of Jesus are for you — hope, joy, peace, and love. In your ordinariness, right where you are, God comes to you. At Christmas time you are somebody.

Luke 2:1-20 (C) Christmas Day/Eve
Luke 2:15-20 (RC)

The Highest In The Lowest

In that region there were shepherds living in the fields, keeping watch over their flocks by night. Then an angel of the Lord stood before them, and the glory of the Lord shone around them, and they were terrified.
— Luke 2:8-9

During a cold winter's night in Bethlehem in the Judean hills, the pains of childbirth came upon Mary. She appears as one more human figure in the eternal agony of motherhood amid the harsh, hard conditions of the ancient world. We must not forget the stark realism of the brutally human aspects of this birth. This loving and heavenly atmosphere faced tragic and difficult times. Look closely, for this that surrounds Mary and Joseph is a parable about life with all of its heavenly and human qualities. It is much like our lives, where there is the blending of the heavenly and the earthly, joy and sorrow, anticipation and disappointment.

Heaven Touches The Earth
Look where heavenly glory touches the earth. It happened in the birth of a child on the outskirts of a remote Judean village called Bethlehem. A comparable place to Bethlehem in Florida would be Yeehaw Junction or Sopchoppy. That's how remote the

location of this birth happened to be. The miracle was not so much the pregnancy of a woman who was not living with a man, but that this child should be the Messiah.

At the time of this birth there was no rug on the floor, no costly chandelier, no furniture, no antiseptic labor room, no anesthesiologist, nor crisp, clean linen for the bed. Here the light of God touched the earth as never before. If we translate this birth into twentieth century language, then the Messiah was born in a storage shed behind a motel seventy miles from home with a cardboard box for a bed.

Luke in his narrative will not let us escape the scandal of God's actions. From the beginning to the end, Jesus is an outcast among outcasts for the outcast. The story of this birth from Luke's point of view points out that God has chosen to side with the oppressed against the oppressor. If that is true, it would appear that anyone or any church that has lost sight of human oppression and poverty will certainly lose the full impact of Jesus' birth.

God Comes To Us Where We Are

In our text it was the shepherds who first heard the message about Jesus' birth. Why the shepherds? Because God is to be found in the places of dire human need. The Advent confirms that God comes to us right where we are. God does not ask us to clean ourselves up or to straighten ourselves out. God knows how futilely we have been doing that. The fact is that we can not go where God is, but God comes to us where we are. God comes to us through people with all of their handicaps, ordinariness, and disabilities — especially the disability of poverty. The Advent tells us that God cares for all people. Through Jesus, God is Emmanuel, who comes to us by the roadside in the normal, daily events of everyday life. It is like the woman who in the ordinary activity of her day comes to draw water from the well. In her daily routine she encounters Jesus at the well and her life is forever changed. It is like Matthew sitting in his tax office conducting his business as he does every day. In that normal, ordinary, everyday setting he meets Jesus and follows him, never to return to the office again. The same is true for us. Christ comes to us right where we are, amid all of our human entanglements. It is hard for us to think of God in such ordinary terms.

God — So Near And So Ordinary

This is exactly why the hometown folks in Mark 6 had such difficulty in accepting Jesus as Messiah. He was too much like them. If this was God, then God was too ordinary. They spoke up and said, "We know who he is. He is not fooling us. That's the carpenter's son. That's Joseph's boy." This meant that he was from the side streets of Nazareth. He was from the industrial park area where he lived over the carpenter shop with his family. Immediately, this brings to our minds train tracks, warehouses, cement mixers, asphalt plants, signs, and billboards. They said among themselves, "He is from the lower order. What does he know?"

You see, they had the facts on him. They knew his origin, his family, his name, and occupation. There are those who, knowing the origin of someone, are convinced they understand all there is to know about that person. They are convinced that people from certain locations, races, cultures, or backgrounds are all alike and that no one of any importance can come from those kinds of roots. We have heard it all before, haven't we? As far as Jesus is concerned, they had the facts on him, but they did not really know him.

That day in Nazareth they stumbled over the truth because it appeared so ordinary, so obvious and familiar. Fred Craddock tells how, upon the death of a saint, those who visited his home after his death were surprised to find a broom, detergents, trash cans, old newspapers, an ironing board, dirty dishes, a worn sweater, toilet tissue, a can of tuna, Sweet and Low, and utility bills. With astonishment they gasped, "He was just like us!" How hard it is for us to realize that liberation comes to us on limping, human feet! The highest comes to us amid the lowest.

Christ In Others

Leo Tolstoy tells the story of a cobbler, whose name was Conrad, a godly man who made shoes in his humble shop. One night the cobbler dreamed that the next day Jesus was coming to his shop. He got up early the next morning and went to the woods to gather green boughs to decorate his shop in order to receive so great a guest.

He waited all morning and the only thing that happened was that an old man shuffled up, asking to rest. Conrad saw that his shoes were worn through, so he brought the man in. "I'll give you a new pair of shoes," he said and put on the old man the sturdiest shoes in the shop before sending him on his way.

He waited through the afternoon and the only happening was that an old woman under a heavy load of firewood came by. She was weary and, out of compassion, Conrad brought her in and gave her some of the food he had prepared for his special, anticipated guest. She ate with relish, for she was hungry. Refreshed, she went on her way.

As night came a lost child, crying bitterly, into his shop. The cobbler was annoyed by the child's presence, because he felt it necessary to leave his shop and take the child to his home. As he returned to his shop he was convinced that he had missed his Lord.

Sadly, he sat down, and in his imagination he lived through the moments with Jesus as he imagined they might have been. He thought to himself, "What a great time it could have been."

Conrad cried, "Why is it, Lord, that your feet have delayed in coming? Have you forgotten that this was the day?" Then softly in the silence a voice was heard:

> *Lift up your heart for I kept my word.*
> *Three times I came to your friendly door;*
> *Three times my shadow was on your floor.*
> *I was a beggar with bruised feet;*
> *I was the woman you gave to eat;*
> *I was the child on the homeless street.*

The highest comes in the lowest.

How are things with you this Christmas? Is it possible you have no sense of the nearness and the presence of God? For you angels' voices are never heard and the thrill of the high and the holy never enters your life. Nothing about Christmas really grabs you. You are having a hard time really catching the spirit of the season. It could be that you have been looking in the wrong place. It is not to be found in what you receive but in what you give.

Martin of Tours was a Roman soldier and a deeply committed Christian who lived in France in the fourth century. The story has it that early one winter morning he was met by a beggar who was shivering and blue from the cold. Without hesitation Martin took off his army cloak and wrapped it around the beggar's shoulders. That night he had a dream. In it he saw a vast multitude gathered in heaven and Jesus stood among them, clad in a Roman army cloak. One of the angels asked, "Lord, where did you get that Roman army cloak?" Jesus answered softly, "My servant Martin gave it to me."

This Advent Jesus stands among us, although disguised. If you turn away the addict, the beggar, the elderly, the lonely, the refugee, or the powerless, you may be turning away Jesus. To meet your neighbor or a stranger at the level of his or her need is to meet Jesus. It is possible that the highest and the holiest come to us in the least and lowest.

Luke 2:22-40   Christmas 1

Discovering The Unexpected

Simeon took him in his arms and praised God, saying, "Master, now you are dismissing your servant in peace, according to your word; for my eyes have seen your salvation."
— Luke 2:28-30

Have you ever looked forward to something and when it happened, it was so much more than you anticipated? Maybe this was your experience at the time of your marriage or the birth of your first child. This was somewhat like the experience of David Livingstone, the explorer and missionary to central Africa in the mid-1800s. In his journal he tells about his discovery of the great falls, which he named the Victoria Falls, and what that experience meant to him. He had heard from the natives that there was something up the river, but he was not sure what it was. He could hear the roar of the falls for miles and he could see the spray five miles away. He said he could never explain the splendor that fell upon his soul when he looked on the falls for the first time. Suddenly, right before his eyes, the Zambezi River was a mile wide; it sloped slightly and then cascaded in a 400-foot plunge in a display of awesome splendor. He said for several minutes the sight literally paralyzed him. He knew that something was ahead but his discovery was far beyond his wildest imagination.

This is exactly what happened to Simeon in the text. He knew the Messiah was coming and he waited and prayed for the day to arrive. He was told by the Holy Spirit that he would not see death until he would see the Lord's Messiah. Every time parents brought their children to the Temple he was filled with anticipation that possibly one of them was the child he was waiting for. Then Mary and Joseph arrived at the Temple and Simeon, now an old man, took the child up into his arms and praised God saying:

> *Master, now you are dismissing your servant in peace, according to your word; for my eyes have seen your salvation, which you have prepared for all peoples.*

The scene is a moving one: an old man now ready to die holding a six-week-old baby, who is at long last "the salvation for all people."

Exceeding Expectations

The joy of Simeon's discovery exceeded his expectations. He did not know what it all meant, which is true of anyone who makes such a great discovery. I am certain that Columbus had no idea of the magnitude of his discovery or that he was opening a whole new world. It never dawned on the Wright brothers that they were the pioneers of space travel. Little did Simeon know that the child he held in his arms was to have such a dramatic and forceful impact on the course of human history. But he did know that something great and significant was taking place and he was part of it.

The fact is Simeon was an exception, because the first century world was not prepared for the coming of this Christ. It is true that the nation of Israel had anticipated the coming of the Messiah for centuries. The whole nation expected him and the fiber of their stories, art, literature, and songs carried this theme for more than 300 years. Because of this expectation they were willing to bear the indignities of exile and Roman occupation. But the birth of Jesus was so unexpected, not as to his coming, but because of the manner of his coming. The Messiah did come, but they did know it, because the manner and the style of Jesus' life was unexpected.

John the Baptist was the first one to raise some doubts when he asked, "Are you the one who is to come, or must we look for another?" The fact that John has such doubts is startling since he had been so close to Jesus. His doubts grew from the fact that Jesus did not fulfill his nationalistic expectations. He was no aggressive deliverer, no majestic and severe Messiah in the sense that he would swiftly smash evil with a mighty sword, chasing all the political foreigners from the land and bringing political freedom from Rome.

Jesus — The Unexpected

He was the unexpected Jesus. They expected him to come with fanfare. He did not. They expected Jesus to bring political freedom from foreign occupation; instead he brought freedom from sin and guilt. They expected a Jesus who would dazzle them by miraculous feats. But instead, he healed the sick, cared for the poor, and fed the hungry. They expected a messiah who would make life easier, reduce taxes, increase employment, and bring down prices. He didn't. If anything, he made life harder. He talked about crosses and not about crowns. He talked about his way of life being harder and the entrance into it as being narrow and that few would enter into it. He talked about loving your enemy and the wrongs others have done to you as God has forgiven you. Those who do not leave all behind and set their minds and hearts on the kingdom of God, he said, are not worthy of him. They expected a Christ who would be a smashing success, but to them he was not because he died the shameful death of a criminal. He was the unexpected Christ because he did not fit into their scheme or plan of things. They wanted a Christ they could keep for themselves exclusively as part of their nation, but his life was like a river, a current so strong that no bank could contain it.

Jesus did not come then where men and women expected him to come. He may not come today where we expect him to come. We have a tendency to look for God to come among us in the bright spots of the world, in the creeds and in the cathedrals. But he was found in the shadows, by the pool of Bethesda with the crippled and the diseased. A man jumped into a cab in New York City and told the cabbie to take him to God. Without hesitation the cabbie drove him to St. Patrick's Cathedral. As the man got out of the cab he asked the driver, "Are you sure that God is here?" "If he is not here, he is not in town," the driver answered. I wonder if it ever entered the mind of the driver to take the man to Bellevue, Harlem, or Washington Square.

Christ Is A Living Presence

Today, Christ comes as an angel that troubles the waters. He comes as he did in the first century — the tormentor of men's and women's souls. We can feel quite satisfied with our lives until Christ comes along. In the day that we confront him we discover we cannot remain as we are. We must either change or flee from his presence. He offends our prejudices and challenges our basic axioms; he reveals our shabby respectability for what it is. Today, he is not a figure of history who lived 2000 years ago. He is not a Christ in a stained glass window. He is not eternally a baby in a manger in Bethlehem. He is a living presence. He is an all-invading Christ, a life-revolutionizing Christ, and for many that is intolerable.

Jesus is saying to us, "You cannot wrap me up in a proof-sheet of logical, rational reasoning. You cannot have me gift-wrapped for a Christmas present. You cannot preserve me in your theological formulas or your religious incitations." The fact is, Christ breaks through all of our notions about him. The dynamic of his life cannot be confined, but he is ever revealing himself in the most unexpected ways.

Jesus Came To Share Our Life

Expected or unexpected, Christ came. The world will never be the same since his coming. He came into the midst of life as the apostle declares in Galatians 4:4 ". . . God sent forth his son, born of a woman, under the law . . ." Buttrick reminds us that Jesus knew our life; like us he was weary at nightfall. His tears were salty like our tears, and when he cut his hand, his blood was red and crimson like our blood. He was a tradesman, who labored in his father's carpenter shop, knew firsthand about irritable customers and at times found it hard to collect his bills and make ends meet.

He craved human friendship. He shared in the anguish of parents over the death of their child; he suffered in the despair of the unemployed in the market place. He knew the plight of the poor and the shame of the outcast. He identified with the "undesirables." He grieved over the stubbornness of men and women. He laughed with little children. He died bleeding, but not before he had felt our ultimate doubt when he cried, "My God, my God, why have you forsaken me?" He "was crucified, dead and buried" — a phrase which is the creed's blunt testimony to his humanness. That Jesus came to share our lives there is no doubt.

We can look out at the bewildering and terrifying conditions in our world today and say as the Christmas hymn states: "Jesus Christ is born for this." This Christmas will not be the same for some of you. The loss of a loved one has greatly altered your life, but "Jesus Christ was born for this." Some of you will leave this service and rush back to the side of a loved one, where you have been keeping a faithful vigil. For others this year has been one of misfortune or business and financial reversal; for others, the deterioration of a relationship with your family or marriage. "Jesus Christ was born for this."

Today the world is on the dizzy edge of disarray. Today millions of refugees roam the earth and there are more homeless than ever before. Today we need to lift our voices and sing:

> *Good Christian friends, Rejoice*
> *With heart and soul and voice,*
> *Christ has opened the heavenly door,*
> *We are blessed forever more,*
> ***Jesus Christ Was Born For This.***

John 1:1-18					Christmas 2

God Is Down To Earth

And the Word became flesh and lived among us....
— John 1:14

William Barclay is convinced that John wrote the fourth gospel for the sake of this fourteenth verse. Early in the first chapter John talked about the Word: the creative and dynamic word. The Word was the agent bringing about creation.

> *In the beginning was the Word and the Word was with God, and the Word was God. He was in the beginning with God; all things were made through him, and without him was not anything made that was made.*
> — John 1:3

In the beginning it was this directing, controlling Word which put order in the universe and mind in women and men. John states an incredible, startling fact unheard of in his first century world: the Word, the power, the dynamic, the reason that orders and controls the world "has become flesh and dwells among us." John goes on to say that "we have seen with our eyes . . . and touched with our hands . . . the word of life" (1 John 1:1-2). John's message is that this Word has come to the earth in human form. God, who was so distant, is now near. John is saying that if you want to see what this creating Word, this dynamic power, this controlling reason looks like — look at Jesus of Nazareth. "... In him was life, and the life was the light of all people" (John 1:4).

Leonard Griffith, the outstanding pastor in Toronto, tells the story of a mother who was putting her little daughter to bed in the midst of a thunderstorm. She told her daughter that she did not need to be frightened, that her mother and father were close by in the living room. The girl replied to her mother, "Mommy, but when it thunders this way, I want somebody who has skin on." This simple, homely story, in essence, is the essential truth of our text. The invisible spirit of God did clothe himself in skin, flesh, and blood and came to dwell among us with grace and truth.

God Has Put On Flesh

Prior to the coming of Christ there were those who acknowledged that they had seen God. This was at best a partial, rather general revelation of God. For the writer of Psalm 8 there was the knowledge of God in nature. For Israel there was the knowledge of God through history. God was seen in their hearts. But in Christ, God became clothed in human flesh. People now see God with their eyes. God has put on skin. God is down to earth.

God Is Approachable

Now that Word has been uttered by a human being, who lived among us like other human beings. Now a human being shows us the splendor of divine nature in terms of a personal character and social action, and finds us where we live. In other words, in Jesus Christ, God is down to earth.

The best people, the most useful and helpful people, are down-to-earth people. Abraham Lincoln was known for his leadership in uniting a divided nation. What the people loved about Lincoln, was his down-to-earth nature. He identified with common people. He was approachable. Carl Sandburg, in his biography of Lincoln, tells how on certain days each month the people were invited to the White House to bring their concerns to the President. The people came because they were convinced that their president cared about them. It was Lincoln who said, "God must have loved the common people, because he made so many of them." Above all he was approachable and had time for them, an utter impossibility for a president today.

Desmond Tutu is a brilliant Anglican bishop in South Africa. He could have withdrawn to the ivy towers of academia and even there gain notoriety. But the world respects Desmond Tutu because of his willingness to be a down-to-earth bishop who stood with blacks in Soweto until apartheid was finally overcome.

Albert Schweitzer, in a sense, was a high-brow man. He had earned doctor of philosophy and medical degrees, as well as being an authority on Bach and a master at the organ. The world appreciated him, not for his intellectual capacity, but for being down-to-earth in his servanthood to the people of Africa.

The world's memorable people are not only talented, but down-to-earth and approachable. In Christ, God is approachable. It was by the incarnation that God came to the earth, becoming accessible to all.

This text, John 1:14, about the Word becoming flesh and dwelling among us with grace and truth, is often heard, but seems to have little meaning to our ears. It contains a basic truth but it is one that we seem to stumble over. It contains not only a basic truth, but a mystery. It is difficult for us to accept the fact that God is so down-to-earth, that God should come to us on such human and ordinary terms. We are astonished at God's availability.

What's So Great About Jesus?

I had the opportunity to attend the morning worship service at Madison Avenue Presbyterian Church in New York City and to hear David H.C. Read preach just before his retirement. He told the story of a grandmother in his church who wanted her grandson to attend Sunday School. One Sunday she arranged to pick him up and bring him to Sunday School with her. On the way home she was anxious to hear what he had to say about his Sunday School experience, so she asked him, "How did things go this morning?"

He thought for a moment and then he said to her, "Grandma, what's so great about Jesus?" Hearing this, I thought: that's what Christmas is all about — telling our children and our grandchildren what is so great about Jesus. A mother told me after church one Sunday during Advent that she asked her son what Christmas was all about. She said she was holding her breath waiting for his reply, thinking that it might include merely the receiving of gifts and Santa Claus. Without the slightest hesitation he said, "It is the birthday of Jesus." She was so happy, she hugged him.

Norman Cousins, in telling about his visit with Albert Schweitzer, described the regular after-dinner ritual in the African jungle hospital at Lambarene. Cousins said the great doctor would announce the hymn to be sung and then sit down at the old upright piano to play. Cousins said that the piano was at least fifty years old. The keyboard was badly stained. One or more strings were missing on a dozen keys. The jungle heat and moisture made its tuning almost impossible. This great interpreter of Bach's organ music sat down to play this dilapidated old instrument. To Cousin's amazement the old instrument seemed to lose its poverty in Schweitzer's hands. Its capacity to yield music was now being fully realized. For whatever reason, Schweitzer's presence at the piano seemed to make it right.

What is so great about Jesus? He takes human character, regardless of how broken or dilapidated, as long as it is sensitive to his touch, and he brings out the best in it. That's what is so great about Jesus! He can heal our broken lives. He can bring harmony out of disharmony. He can repair the damaged human instrument. He restores its strength, its resilience, and its capacity to yield noble and joyous music.

God Became Domesticated in Jesus

By means of the incarnation, God becoming flesh, God has come into the midst of life. Jesus knew life as we know it. He was raised in a family as the elder son was eventually responsible for caring for his widowed mother. He knew what it was for one's friends to turn against him, to be falsely accused and to suffer rejection and finally a cruel death. E. Stanley Jones has suggested that in Jesus Christ God became domesticated. He knew life as we know life. Therefore, in the midst of our anguish, pain, and disappointment, we can cry out and say, "Lord, you know how it is!" God does. For God had a son who lived among us full of grace and truth.

The Word of God became flesh in Jesus Christ! This fact is driven home to us as we take the bread and the cup at the Lord's table. In this mystery of holy communion the love of Christ seeks to become flesh in us. There are within this text of John 1:14 subtle tones of a sacramental theology that give meaning to this Gospel of the incarnation. The English poet John Betman is helpful to us when he writes:

> *No love that in a family dwells,*
> *No caroling in frosty air,*
> *Nor all the steeple-shaking bells,*
> *Can with this simple Truth compare.*
> *That God was Man in Palestine*
> *And lives today in bread and wine.*

When things in this world appear out of control, when disappointment and despair grip your heart, when friends let you down and circumstances appear overwhelming, remember: "The Word of God has become flesh and lives among us full of grace and truth."

Mark 1:4-11 (C)   Epiphany 1
Mark 1:7-11 (RC)   (Baptism Of The Lord)

A Moment Of Decision

In those days Jesus came from Nazareth of Galilee and was baptized by John in the Jordan.
— Mark 1:9

Experiences have the effect of changing the direction of our lives. These experiences are so casual they are frightening. They are critical experiences because they are life-changing. Albert Schweitzer casually walked into a library and sat down at a table to study. He picked up a magazine that someone had failed to return to the rack. It was a publication of the London Missionary Society. As he thumbed through it, an article about African missions caught his eye. That article changed the direction of his life. He could have been a great organist, performing in the world's most renowned concert halls, or a medical doctor, working in the great research centers of the world. Instead, he would spend the rest of his life in Lambarene, Africa, as a Christian missionary, all because of a casual visit to a library. Some of the weightiest decisions of our lives can turn on the tiniest of hinges.

Life-changing Events

Have you ever had a similar experience? It is not the ostentatious or the loud events, but those that are casual. At the time they are happening you don't give them a second thought. Often those are the events that bring the most profound change. Suddenly, things seem to converge and you meet new people or get a new idea or acquire a different way of looking at things. The results are life-changing.

This is what happened to Jesus at the time of his baptism. John the Baptist declared, "I baptize you with water, but he who is mightier than I is coming and he will baptize you with the Holy Spirit and fire." John's coming was for Jesus a sign, a turning point, a moment of decision.

This incident in the life of Jesus made sense to the early Christians because it expressed so fully an essential element in their own personal experience of God. This story contains the voice of the Father, the presence of the Son, and the promptings of a gentle dove-like Spirit. This was their own experience of God. This is why this story made so much sense to them. These same things are true for us and our experience of God.

Several things in Jesus' baptism are analogous to our lives. One such thing that stands out is the delay. Jesus had been waiting for thirty years for this to take place. For thirty years he had waited for John to come preaching and baptizing. It must have seemed to Jesus that this time would never come. It appeared that his public ministry would never happen. Luke tells us that "Jesus was about thirty years old when he began his work" (3:23). Since life expectancy in the first century was barely forty, this was late in coming. Delays are difficult for us. We interpret God's delays as God's denials. There are those times when we feel that life has passed us by. Today, I simply want to indicate what this baptism meant to Jesus and what it implies for us who are committed to him.

A Turning Point

First, why was Jesus baptized? This moment was a turning point in Jesus' life. It ended forever his life in Nazareth. He was to begin his public ministry. We know very little about these early years. There is evidence that his father died when he was a young man. As the eldest son he cared for the family and took over the family business and ran the carpenter shop in Nazareth. There is some thought that he was a skilled craftsman like his father. One New Testament scholar has suggested that there might have been a sign over his carpenter shop which read, "My Yoke is Easy," indicating that his yokes were so skillfully crafted that they fit perfectly over the shoulders of the oxen, causing no chafing and making heavy burdens light.

John came preaching a baptism of repentance. His message declared that God's judgment was imminent. The only way people could escape it was to confess their sins and in a deliberate act of repentance turn from their wrongdoing. But surely Jesus had no need to be baptized under those conditions. Why then was Jesus baptized by John? There seems to be only one answer. These were the people that Jesus came to save. The only way to save them and reveal his love for them was to get alongside of them. Jesus felt the need to identify with them. He got down in the water alongside these men and women and identified with their need. Jesus also wanted to identify with John both in his message and in his preaching. These seem to be the logical reasons for Jesus' baptism by John that day in the Jordan.

Baptism Is A Decisive Moment

Isn't this what we have been celebrating at Christmas time? God became flesh and knew life exactly as we know it. The whole of Jesus' ministry after the baptism and his identification with us is consistent with the incarnation. Jesus did not stand aloof from human involvement. He entered into all areas of life, accepting the hospitality of those whom the religious leaders regarded as contaminated and unfit. He was accused of being the friend of the publicans and sinners. He did this in defiance of the Jewish law which said that good men kept their hands clean and avoided notorious sinners like the plague. Not Jesus. He deliberately went to them and offered God's forgiveness and the chance for a new life. This complete identification with sinners begins at Jesus' baptism and continues all the way to the cross.

Afterwards, Jesus heard the words, "This is my beloved Son." These words are taken from Psalm 2, a psalm used at the coronation of a king. As the king was crowned and oil poured on his head, the words were said, "You are my son, today I have begotten you" (Psalm 2:7). The king became the messiah. So at this moment Jesus is assured by God that he is the Messiah. This was his coronation. Beyond any shadow of doubt his relationship to God his father is now confirmed with the words, "This is my beloved Son." There may be moments that Jesus would wonder about what is transpiring in his life, but he could look back upon this moment and draw upon its reality and strength. Although he may have had doubts, he would never doubt his call.

The words that followed, "with whom I am well pleased," must have had a tremendous effect on him. The words came from Isaiah 42, a passage in which Isaiah describes the character and mission of God's messiah. According to Isaiah, he would be a servant, but more than that, he would be a suffering servant, taking upon himself the consequences and the punishment of the sins of others. This baptism experience certainly did give meaning and direction to Jesus' public ministry which was about to begin.

At his baptism by John in the river Jordan, the decisive moment in Jesus' life finally arrived. He left his hometown, his family, and friends, and launched out on that mission for which his whole life was directed. To use a good New Testament word, this was his *kairos*, his time. The Greek language has two words for time: *kairos*, which means a point in time; and *chronos*, which means a long period of time. This is where we get our word *chronology*. Jesus' baptism was his *kairos*, a critical moment, a decisive moment. He is no longer the waiting messiah or the eldest son caring for the family business. Now, in the words of John, he is "the lamb of God, who takes away the sin of the world."

Jesus Begins His Ministry

What does the baptism of Jesus mean for us today? One thing that stands out for us in the story of Jesus' baptism is that, after a long delay, Jesus' public ministry finally began. It is hard to wait and be patient. We are so used to having things done immediately. We live in a world of the instant — no delays or waiting. But God is in no hurry. We live and work in the framework of time, and

God's framework is eternity. We do not handle delays very well. Patience is not one of our virtues. The words of Howard Thurmond are meaningful:

> *Always I have an underlying anxiety about things,*
> *Sometimes I am in a hurry to achieve my ends*
> *And am completely without patience. It is hard*
> *For me to realize*
> *That some growth is slow,*
> *That all processes are not swift. I cannot always discriminate*
> *Between what takes time to develop and what can*
> *Be rushed,*
> *Because my sense of time is dulled.*
> *I measure things in terms of happenings.*
> *O, to understand the meaning of perspective*
> *That I may do all things with a profound sense of leisure.*[1]

For several years I have served on the Board of the Ordained Ministry. This board is responsible for the preparedness of candidates for ministry. We are now seeing older men and women who are already established in a career coming before the board as candidates for ministry. They have grown tired of climbing that corporate ladder of success and they are convinced that there is more to life. At this later period they have had the call to the ordained ministry. They have discovered an all-consuming purpose for their lives. They all express amazement that it took so long for them to discover such a deep sense of fulfillment for their lives. This reminds all of us to pray and be patient. The Lord has not given up on us.

Baptized Into Jesus' Ministry

What does the baptism of Jesus mean for us today? Simply, it means that the way we live in the world and the kind of service that we do is the same for us as it was for Jesus. We have been baptized into Christ and into his ministry. The pattern of our life must be one of involvement in the world and identification with people in need. We cannot escape the hard fact that this will be a costly experience and could lead to suffering. The apostle reminds us, "... if, in fact, we suffer with him so that we may also be glorified with him" (Romans 8:17).

To be baptized into this ministry of Jesus means involvement on our part. It is at this point we are afflicted with paralysis. We talk a good thing rather than doing a good thing. When discussing his success in sports Deion Sanders, the flamboyant athlete who played both professional football and baseball, said, "You can't just talk the talk; you gotta walk the walk." Success is more than mere words. Many times we Christians get caught up by the delusion of glowing words and statements. Many feel that if they have talked about something or approved a definitive report on the problem, then they have done their job. In our churches we have our endless synods, forums, conferences, and seminars which on so many occasions are unrelated to the real world around us. If mere words and meetings would solve the world's problems, then the church could have accomplished this a long time ago. We need to do more than "talk the talk." We've got to "walk the walk."

In Petrograd, Russia, in 1916, the leaders of the Russian Orthodox Church were involved in a heated discussion regarding liturgy and vestments. At the same time in the same building, the Bolsheviks were planning a revolution. The church leaders were so out of touch that the revolution swept away both the Czar and the church. The church is not a place for refuge, to get away from the cares and burdens of modern life. It is not a modern Noah's ark. Our baptism calls us to the ministry of involvement as it did Jesus. Through our baptism we are called to bring the might and the power of the Gospel to bear on every aspect of human life. We cannot do that if we stand aloof, unrelated to the world.

In our baptism, we identify with others as Christ has identified with us. We willingly become the hands of Christ to do the work of love and reconciliation.

---

1. Howard Thurman, *Deep Is The Hunger* (Harper and Row, 1973), p.72.

John 1:43-51 (C)
John 1:35-42 (RC)

Epiphany 2
Ordinary Time 2

Pass It On

Philip found Nathanael and said to him, "We have found him whom Moses in the law and also the prophets wrote, Jesus son of Joseph from Nazareth. Nathanael said to him, "Can anything good come out of Nazareth?" Philip said to him, "Come and see."
— John 1:45-46

Here we see the dynamic of witness. Look at what took place. Jesus met Philip and he called him, and Philip followed Jesus. Philip was much like Andrew; he could not keep a secret. When Andrew discovered Jesus, he ran to find his brother and said to him, "Come, Peter. I have found the Messiah." So with the same manner of enthusiasm, Philip went and found his friend Nathanael. He told Nathanael that he was sure that this was the Messiah. But Nathanael was skeptical. He was probably skeptical for several reasons. William Barclay has pointed out that there was nothing in the Old Testament that suggested the Messiah would come from Nazareth (*John*, Vol. 1, p. 78). As far as Nathanael was concerned, Nazareth was not the kind of place where anything good was likely to be found. There is no doubt that Nazareth was quite an undistinguished place. But Philip did not agree with Nathanael. He merely said, "Come and see." Nathanael, because of Philip's invitation, came and saw.

The Pattern Of Witness

As we have noted, there is a similarity between Philip finding Nathanael and Andrew finding Peter. But there is a major difference. This is the first time in chapter one that testimony to Jesus is met with resistance. Gail O'Day points out that Nathanael's resistance highlights the tension that is inherent in Philip's witness (*The New Interpreter's Bible*, Vol. 9, p. 532). Philip does not argue with Nathanael. Instead he offers the same invitation to Nathanael that Jesus extends to his first disciples (v. 39b). Philip wants Nathanael to come and see and then to decide for himself whether this human (son of Joseph) from Nazareth is really the Messiah or not.

The words by Jesus in v. 50 are not a rebuke to Nathanael but rather a promise. These words are similar to the words of Jesus in the story of Thomas (John 20:29). Jesus does not criticize Nathanael's skepticism, but suggests that Nathanael is merely at the beginning point of his faith. The main point of this narrative seems to be that Philip was a faithful witness to Jesus regarding Nathanael. Because of Philip's willingness to "pass it on" Nathanael found the one who satisfied his waiting, longing, and seeking heart.

Nathan Williams told of two men who had been business partners for over twenty years met one Sunday morning as they were leaving a restaurant. One of them asked, "Where are you going this morning?" "I'm going to play golf. What about you?" the other replied. The first man responded rather apologetically, "I'm going to church." The other man said, "Why don't you give up that church stuff?" The man asked, "What do you mean?" "Well," said the other, "we have been partners for twenty years. We have worked together, attended board meetings together, and had lunch together, and all of these twenty years you have never talked to me about going to church. You have never invited me to go with you. Obviously, it doesn't mean that much to you."

I am impressed by that story. The logic is irresistible. If Christ is the joy of life and through your contact with him you have new experience of wonder and light, so that the old, gray, monotonous world has given way to a life of joy, peace, power, and love for others, then surely you should long to pass it on to others. Philip made a great discovery. He found the Messiah. He could not keep this discovery to himself. He ran to find his friend Nathanael and brought him to Jesus. He had to pass it on.

Enriching Faith by Sharing It
To share one's faith is to enrich one's faith. I enjoy raising flowers. I have learned it is necessary to plant the right flowers, at the right time, in the right place. In central Florida you have to select the right flowers that can withstand the hot summer sun and the rather dry conditions. One flower that does well in the summer is the zinnia. It thrives in the hot summer and provides a magnificent array of beautiful colors. There is one variety of zinnia that is called "Cut and Come Again." It is well-named. When one flower is cut it seems like three blossoms are ready to take its place. The more you cut and give away, the more you have. That is exactly what happens when you share your faith. The more you give away, the more you have. God has given you this treasure to share. By sharing your faith you enrich your faith.

Methodism began as a lay movement. For John Wesley, preaching and testifying belonged to the whole church. At the beginning of the Wesleyan revival, lay people were utilized to spread the gospel. Wesley felt it was a fatal mistake to leave the task of spreading the gospel to the ordained clergy. Witnessing was the task of the whole church. He felt it was heresy to turn the ministry of the Christian church into a clergy-dominated religion. Across the world, church growth is the greatest where the laity are the most involved. The small group movement, which is lay-centered like early Methodism with its class meetings, is putting vitality, vision, and enthusiasm back into the church.

Leslie Weatherhead, the English pastor and psychologist, told about a young, brilliant doctor he met in London who was making a number of experiments in a laboratory that was attached to the university. He was doing cancer research and his work was supported by some of the most distinguished scientists in London. Weatherhead said he watched him work in a small, ill-ventilated room in the basement of the university. The doctor told Weatherhead that if these experiments turned out as successfully as he had every right to hope they would, then he would have a new way of treating this particular cancer with some hope of recovery. Weatherhead asked him, "What will you then do?" With a glow on his face, with enthusiasm in his voice, and a shining gleam in his eye he exclaimed, "I shall tell the world!"

We have come to worship with great expectations. With a glow on our faces, enthusiasm in our voices, and a shining gleam in our eyes, we too have made a discovery. Jesus Christ is Lord and he is among his people. Christ has come to set the captive free. What then? We leave to tell the world, to share our discovery, and to pass it on.

A Witnessing Faith

In a recent Bible study of the Book of Acts it became clear to me that the underlying purpose for the formation of the church is to be a witness to the Gospel. The key verse is 1:8: "But you shall receive power when the Holy Spirit has come upon you; and you shall be my witnesses in Jerusalem, and in all of Judea and Samaria and to the ends of the earth." The following 27 chapters in Acts are the results of that witness. What had started in Jerusalem in the first two chapters, by chapter 28 had spread all the way to Rome, the very center of power and authority. When Peter had completed his great sermon at Pentecost, he made this final statement, "This Jesus God raised up, and of that we all are witnesses" (Acts 2:32). Our New Testament faith is a witnessing faith. D.T. Niles, the bishop from Sri Lanka, defined our witnessing as "one beggar telling another beggar where to find bread."

The Bible teaches us that the "word became flesh." For the word of God to be communicated, it must become flesh. Phillips Brooks, the New England preacher of a century ago, maintained that "truth is expressed through personality." Personality is the vehicle for conveying God's truth. Our task is to spread the good news of God's story, in the light of our own particular story, with the hope that people will respond in faith.

It is through the lives of real people that we see and hear the story of God's redeeming grace. There was a little girl who had a brief line in a Sunday School Christmas program. All she had to say was, "I am the light of the world." She rehearsed it until she knew it by heart. As the program approached she was confident, but her mother was nervous. When the little girl saw all of the people the night of the program she became nervous and forgot her lines. Her mother, who was seated in the front row, tried to prompt her. Carefully and slowly the mother's lips formed the words, "I am the light of the world." The little girl straightened and with a loud, confident voice announced, "My mother is the light of the world." In a real sense, so are we all.

Commitment To Discipleship

Not only did Philip encounter Jesus that day, but later he was called to be a disciple of Jesus Christ. We are called to be disciples. The word "disciple" denotes a call, a commitment (a response to the call), and a discipline (the assuming of a lifestyle). Dietrich Bonhoeffer in his book *The Cost of Discipleship* reminds us that discipleship has a cost, a price tag. How could we ever be a disciple or enter discipleship without discipline? Bonhoeffer talks about how we have sought "cheap grace." In our desire for "cheap grace" we want to be a Christian without discipline, have faith without commitment, participate in communion without confession, and experience baptism without repentance. The results are that our Christian witness is weak and ineffective.

Ron Fraser, who until his retirement last year, was the baseball coach at the University of Miami for over twenty years. He won numerous national championships. He had several opportunities to manage in the majors, but he remained at Miami where he maintained an outstanding record. When he was asked the reason why he was so successful as a baseball manager, his answer was simply, "I teach my players the basics." The basics for him were pitching, fielding, and running the bases. His record speaks for itself.

Successful Christian discipleship is getting back to the basics. John Wesley brought renewal to the Church of England in the eighteenth century by getting back to the basics. He established the class meetings, small groups that follow three basics: prayer, Bible study, and witnessing. Every renewal of the church from then until now has come through the same manner. In our text today, Philip is one of the first persons to ever respond to Jesus' call. The first thing he did following his encounter with Jesus was to witness to his friend about his discovery: "Nathanael, come and see. I have found the Messiah. Let me introduce him to you."

Eight-year-old Benny died of AIDS in 1987. CBS made a movie drama about the trauma called *Moving Toward the Light.* As Benny lies dying in his mother's arms, he asks, "What will it be like?" His mother whispers softly in his ear, "You will see a light, Benny, far away — a beautiful, shining light at the end of a long tunnel. And your spirit will lift you out of your body and start to travel toward the light. And as you go, a veil will be lifted from your eyes, and suddenly, you will see everything...but most of all, you will feel a tremendous sense of love." "Will it take long?" Benny asks. "No," his mother answers, "not long at all. Like the twinkling of an eye." Many families have been devastated by AIDS. Amid the darkness and despair an eight-year-old boy and his mother witnessed to the sustaining power of the light of God's presence. They have touched the lives of a multitude of people.

> *This is the message we have heard from him and proclaim*
> *to you, that God is light and in him is no darkness at all.*
> — 1 John 1:5

Go and pass it on.

Mark 1:14-20　　　　　　　　　　　　Epiphany 3
　　　　　　　　　　　　　　　　　Ordinary Time 3

Drop-Everything-Discipleship

And Jesus said to them, "Follow me and I will make you fish for people." And immediately they left their nets and followed him.
　　　　　　　　　　　　　　　　　— Mark 1:17-18

This text is a statement about a radical discipleship. It needs to be pointed out at the beginning that this reading is the most compact and compressed statement of the gospel expressed anywhere in the New Testament. Leonard Sweet points out, "In these few verses, Jesus' role as an authoritative, compelling, charismatic preacher is defined; the kernel of the gospel message is expressed; and drop-everything-discipleship — the result of seeing Jesus and hearing his message — is described."

The word "immediately" captures our attention. Jesus called Simon, Andrew, James, and John, and immediately they left their nets and followed him. They abandoned their nets, their boats, and their livelihood. They walked away from their old life, their old ways of doing things, their kindred and family.

Taking A Risk

This is a radical and bold move on their part. Why? Why did they do it? It appears that their response is simply and exclusively based on the power of Jesus' personality and message. The call of Jesus is so strong in their lives that all of the encumbrances of their old lives are jettisoned — their boats and nets, their families, their old life and old ways of doing things are abandoned. Immediately, they make this radical move in order to become disciples of this charismatic artisan-preacher. One must keep in mind that one of the purposes of Mark's gospel is to help us understand what it means to be a disciple of Jesus of Nazareth. This story by the Sea of Galilee is part of that story.

But, are they not taking a risk by following someone whose career appears rather shaky? This Jesus of Nazareth is radical, new, and different. He is preaching to the poor and the dispossessed in Galilee who cannot afford the price-of-living in Jerusalem. What are his career prospects? The chances appear rather clear that he will end up like his friend John the Baptist — facing both prison and death.

These four fisherman seem to be taking a calculated risk by following a leader whose future is uncharted, uncertain, and unpredictable. They are forsaking a familiar past for a problematic and uncertain future. That's always a risky business, especially since they are abandoning such a secure career as Galilean fishermen. It was their father's business before them. It would be their children's after them. The Sea of Galilee had abundant fish. It was hard work. But it was good work. It could maintain for them a good, decent living as it had for their fathers and grandfathers and their families. Why would a person turn his back on something so secure? There appears to be only one answer: they believed Jesus' word to be true. They literally took him at his word when he declared, "The time is fulfilled, and the kingdom of God has come near, repent, and believe in the good news" (Mark 1:15). They did so believe.

Belief Involves Action

The call of God in your life may not be as radical, but it can be just as meaningful, nevertheless. For you it may mean forsaking a familiar past for a problematic future — like taking a new job, accepting a new position, moving to a new community, making a career change in mid-life. Life is always presenting us with moments and times of crisis and opportunity. Why did the disciples make such a bold move? They believed Jesus' word. They felt that what he said was true and trustworthy. Belief always involves action on our part. The disciples left their nets, boats, hired servants, and family to follow Jesus. The same is true for us. Our belief involves action on our part also. We can leave the old behind and begin again as new "creatures in Jesus Christ" because we too can take Jesus at his word. His word is trustworthy.

Now Jesus begins his public ministry. He comes preaching the gospel in Galilee, "Repent and believe in the good news." The time has now come for him to build his staff. Who are these men that he has chosen? They are simple folks, not from the schools and colleges, ecclesiastical centers or aristocracy, neither learned nor wealthy. They are fisherman who are used to hard work. They have strong backs, calloused hands, wind-burned cheeks, and sun-bleached hair. When God calls, people should not think so much about who they are, but about what Jesus can make of them. Not what is, but what can be.

The Call To Discipleship

Notice how Jesus called them. He simply said, "Follow me!" It was a personal invitation of himself. They did not follow Jesus because of what he said, but because of who he was. The disciples perceived Jesus' invitation as one full of power and promise. The kingdom of God which Jesus has proclaimed as "at hand" is so vividly alive in him that his words bring that kingdom to life. The simple fishermen respond to Jesus' call to "follow me" as though they already felt the presence and pull of the kingdom. Leonard Sweet points out that Jesus' call is so strong, his invitation to new life as fishers of human hearts and souls so pressing and poignant, that they do not resist at all. The call is so forceful that the results are immediate and complete.

Notice where he called them. It was during a day's work while they were catching fish, hoisting sails, mending nets, and manning oars. The call came not in God's house, not in a secret place, not in a holy place. It came in a secular and public place. In the middle of a day's work "as Jesus passed along the Sea of Galilee." Where do our deepest religious experiences take place? Not in the church but out-of-doors. In T.S. Eliot's "Murder in the Cathedral" the priest bars the doors of the great Church of Canterbury against would-be assailants. Thomas à Becket would not permit it. He shouted, "Unbar the doors. I will not have the house of prayer, the Church of Christ, the sanctuary turned into a fortress. The church shall be open, even to our enemies. Open the doors!" Another story goes that a church member, branded as a sinner, was forbidden to enter the church. He took his problem to the Lord in prayer. "Lord, they won't let me in because I am a sinner." The Lord answered, "I know how you feel. They won't let me in either." It seems that the church of Jesus Christ has become another secret-society organization.

Unlimited Possibilities

When Jesus called Simon and Andrew to "follow me" it was an invitation that called them out from their familiar paths, out from their fishing boats, into a world of unlimited possibilities. Recently, Percy Sutton, a distinguished lawyer from Harlem, spoke to our congregation. He called us out of our comfortable world of acquaintances and relationships. He told us that this should not be something we do just once a year on Human Relations Sunday. We need to broaden our world and get to know someone different than ourselves and share life together throughout the year.

Tom Seaver, the legendary baseball pitcher, once asked Yogi Berra, "What time is it?" Yogi replied, "Do you mean now?" There is an urgency about the gospel. Now is the time to serve the Lord. It is no longer business as usual or politics as usual or economics as usual because it is no longer life as usual. As one commentator of our time has observed, "In fact, life as usual is a big part of our problem. So why is it still religion as usual?" Look around. The whole world is changing. The Spirit is breaking out all over the place. New light is breaking forth in areas that never before gave even the slimmest signs of hope. Jesus, who said, "I am the light of the world," and is the source of both light and hope, says to us, "Follow me."

The Challenge To Follow Jesus

Are you willing to follow Jesus as he calls you into the community-at-large? What would that mean? It would mean as Jesus carried out his ministry in the world, so are we called into the world. He washed dusty and dirty feet. He fed the hungry and healed broken limbs. He opened sightless eyes, cleansed leprous skin, and cared for the homeless and forsaken.

Are we willing to follow Jesus into the work place? What would that mean? No more oppressive relations between employers and employees. No unjust labor practices. No sexual harassment. No gender discrimination.

Are you willing to follow Jesus into the midst of your home? What would that mean? It would mean significant changes. More equality between husbands and wives. More shared responsibilities. Openness and honesty. It would be risky because it would bring an end to "life as usual." It would bring new direction, a new sense of purpose, along with understanding and hope.

Are you willing to follow Jesus? This is a good time for us to sing together the chorus:

> *I have decided to follow Jesus*
> *I have decided to follow Jesus*
> *No turning back, no turning back*
> *Though none go with me, yet I will follow*
> *No turning back, no turning back.*

Mark 1:21-28 Epiphany 4
Ordinary Time 4

By What Authority?

They were all amazed, and they kept on asking one another, "What is this? A new teaching — with authority!"
— Mark 1:27

Two remarkable things happened. Jesus' words in the synagogue left the people amazed. His confronting of the man with the unclean spirit left them dumbfounded.

Jesus' world was a demon-haunted world. Men and women in the ancient world believed in demons. Demons for them were intensely real. The first century world was one of pain and suffering. There was no relief from pain. It was a world of natural disasters that took a heavy toll on life. Disease, even the slightest illness, could be fatal. There was a high rate of infant mortality. Life expectancy was in the middle forties. Because they had no idea of the causes of natural disaster, calamity, or disease, they associated them with demons. It is difficult for our modern world to realize the power and influence that demons had upon first century human life.

But when it comes to evil and demons, is there that much difference between the first and twentieth centuries? We cannot dismiss evil as a first century phenomenon. It operates as an active force in our world as well as in our souls. In a real sense, in a tragic sense, our world is a "demon-haunted world." We can talk about barbaric acts of cruelty in the hostile and violent ancient world, but similar acts of human brutality have been produced in our day, on our streets, in our homes. It is far more tragic, because today it is done on such a larger scale. Does it appear to you, or is it just part of my imagination, that the latest acts of brutality and evil seem to go one step beyond the one previous to it?

Evil As A Destructive Force

It was in the mid-twentieth century that someone said, "You put the Zygion gas in the cylinders. I'll make sure the doors are closed and the vents are sealed." Someone in this century gave the command at Auschwitz. They were cold, detached words. They were barbarous and cruel, and precipitated an act of brutality that defies description.

"Look out! Tanks have broken through! Tear gas is seeping in! Here, you take the kerosene. Go that way. You go this way. Here's the torch." Someone at Waco gave the command. An inferno erupted. Was this an act in the barbaric, demon-haunted ancient world? Hardly.

"This is the street. Turn left and proceed slowly. Pull up to the entrance of the building. Get as close as possible. Set the timer. Let's get out of here. All hell is about to break loose." An explosion rocks Oklahoma City. One hundred and seventy men, women and children are blown to pieces. A barbaric action of human destruction conceived, planned, and carried out by the human will that is controlled by a destructive force, seeking to tear down what is good and decent, determined to make one less than human.

In my lifetime I have witnessed the Holocaust of World War II, genocide in Cambodia, Jonestown, ethnic cleansing in Bosnia, child abuse in America, Branch Davidians, and the bombings at New York's Twin Towers and Oklahoma City. Who would deny that our century is not possessed of an evil spirit?

Look how powerfully destructive an evil spirit like greed can be when it is let loose in human life. Our environment is suffering from economic exploitation resulting from greed. A passion for wealth has produced a disregard for the world of nature and human survival. Greed can be so destructive to human life. Tonya Harding is a talented and gifted figure skater who competed recently for an Olympic gold metal. She was surrounded by vultures who wanted a share in the pot of gold that she might win at Lillehammer. Her mother, who had been married seven times, stood at rink-side with a hair brush to beat her daughter if her performance fell short of her expectations. Tonya's ex-husband, a hoodlum, helped to concoct a bizarre attack on Tonya's chief competitor, Nancy Kerrigan. The story, which captured national attention for weeks, ended like most stories of greed. The characters self-destructed and the pot of gold vanished. Joseph Conrad reminds us that "the belief in the supernatural source of evil is not necessary. Men alone are quite capable of every wickedness."

Jesus Confronts An Evil Spirit

Jesus came to Capernaum. It was a small, poor village several miles from Jerusalem. It was the Sabbath day, and as was his custom he entered the synagogue for worship and prayer. He had an opportunity for teaching and the people were "astonished" at his words. The word "astonishing" prompts a question: Are we sufficiently "astonished" at Jesus' teaching? The reason we do not "astonish" the world more may be that we are not sufficiently "astonished" ourselves. If we were more "astonished" we would do more "astonishing" things. They were "astonished" at Jesus' teachings, because he taught them as one who had "authority."

Suddenly, there was a commotion. A man with an unclean spirit cried out, "What have you to do with us, Jesus of Nazareth? Have you come to destroy us? I know who you are, the Holy One of God." Jesus must have been startled. The people were spellbound. Silence prevailed. Everyone was looking at Jesus, breathlessly waiting for his reply. Was this an interruption or an amplification of what Jesus had been teaching? Have you ever noticed how in our teaching we are interrupted by the very things we are teaching. I left church after service on a Sunday morning and had just sat down with the family for dinner. I was rudely interrupted by a knock at the door. I opened the door and discovered a forlorn-looking man who asked me, "Excuse me, but do you have anything to do with the church?" I don't know exactly how to answer a question like that. It was obvious by his appearance that he was in need of help. I could have said, "Look, my friend, I just preached two great sermons on Christian commitment. I can't be bothered with you." That was a perfect test of what I had just been talking about.

Relating Belief To Practice

At church we sing "O how I love Jesus." We go home and discover the stewardship commitment card has arrived in the mail. It is then that we change our tune to "Jesus paid it all." No sooner do you leave church than you are confronted with the very things that church is all about — love, generosity, forgiveness, acceptance. Wham! There you are confronting these things right before your very eyes. Someone has said this is where the rubber hits the road. Jesus is interrupted in his lesson of powerful and authoritative teaching by a screaming man with an unclean spirit. The power of Jesus' speech, words, and teaching are transferred to the power of his life to reach out to a desperate man. Jesus' power works for good among those caught in the grip of evil who lack the power to overcome evil by themselves. This is where Jesus gained his authority. He practiced what he preached. He had authority because he connected faith with ethics and belief with practice. What would have happened if, after that great teaching, he could not assist this man and left him possessed of an evil and unclean spirit? The crowd and the disciples would have just drifted away. Jesus would have become just one more among so many. But Jesus' authority is to be found in his ability to back up his words and teaching with action. Jesus had the authority to do what he said he would do. Why doesn't the world take the church seriously? Because we fail to practice what we preach.

What is significant about this story that took place on the Sabbath in that synagogue in Capernaum? Jesus healed a man possessed of an evil and unclean spirit. Why is that so significant? Because it brings hope to us. Paul Tournier, the Swiss doctor and counselor, stated, "Doubtless there are many doctors who in their struggle against disease have had, like me, the feeling that they were confronting not something passive, but a clever and resourceful enemy." Jesus met that enemy that day at Capernaum. He won!

Mark 1:29-39　　　　　　　　　　　Epiphany 5
　　　　　　　　　　　　　　　　Ordinary Time 5

The Demanding Crowd

And the whole city was gathered around the door.
　　　　　　　　　　　　　— John 1:33

　　Jesus was mobbed by the crowds. Because he taught with authority and healed those possessed of an unclean or evil spirit, the crowds sought him out. Everyone with an ailment joined the demanding and pressing mob of people. The text tells us that the entire city was at his doorstep. The crowds came with their brokenness and said, "Fix me." People who were sick, hopeless, and desperate came to him because he offered a glimmer of hope in a hopeless and dismal world.
　　The demanding crowds came because they wanted something. They did not come to capture a new vision for life. They did not come to seek the kingdom of God. They came for one reason, the reason that most crowds come: to get something. They came because he had what they wanted most. He had what they could not find anywhere else — health of mind and body. Wholeness.
　　Most who seek God do so during crisis. For every prayer of thanksgiving and praise offered to God there are ten offered as demands and requests. God often hears the words, "Lord, get me out of this mess and I'll serve you the rest of my life." Does that

sound familiar to you? Those who never pray to God when the sun is shining begin to pray when the clouds come and the cold winds of adversity blow. For most people religion is a "crisis affair." However, there is much to be said about the fact that God is not one to be remembered only in misfortune, but every day of our lives. The remarkable thing is: *regardless of how or when we come — God is there!*

The Need to Withdraw

The demand of the crowd upon Jesus' life was great. So much so that "in the morning, while it was still very dark, he got up and went out to a deserted place, and there he prayed" (John 1:35). Jesus realized he could not give out to others anymore. He went someplace where he could be alone, away from the cries of the needy, the demands of people, the insistence that he do something. Jesus was not trying to get away from the demands of the people or to dodge his responsibilities. It wasn't that he was uncaring about the needs of others or those that surrounded him. Rather it was a matter of staying connected with the Father so that he could maintain a clear sense of purpose.

How easy it is for our lives to be cluttered with the needs and demands of others. We find ourselves going in several different directions at one time. We end up doing a lot of things, but there is no sense of fulfillment or accomplishment. We find ourselves on the edge of burnout. It has been pointed out that burnout is not the result of too much activity. It is the result of the wrong kind of activity. Instead of energizing us and building us up, it wears us down and saps our energy. Jesus needed time to get away and put things in perspective and to gain a clear understanding of God and God's purpose. If Jesus needed to do this, how much more do we need to do it? There is always that possibility that we are busy doing the wrong thing. We need to do what Jesus did — get away and spend time in prayer with God, meditate, and seek God's will, instead of always responding to the demands and needs of others.

Determining The Nature Of Ministry

There are several important factors in this passage. First, Jesus was not going to allow the demands of the crowd to determine the nature and purpose of his ministry. When the crowds were beginning to gather and Jesus was nowhere to be found, his disciples came looking for him. They found that his bed was empty. The text tells us that they went "hunting" for him. Finally they tracked him down and they gave to him what they considered a favorable report: "Everyone is searching for you." They felt that Jesus' responsibility was to comply with the wishes of the crowd. This is the same mistake that the church makes. Too often we convince ourselves that our responsibility is to comply with the demands of the crowd. But the demands of the crowd and the demands of the gospel can often be different demands. This is the most glaring shortcoming of the church growth movements. God is treated like a commodity to be marketed. The church allows the crowd to determine its marketability and to package it in a manner that makes it attractive for public consumption. But God and the gospel are so much more. The message of the gospel often is not what the crowds want to hear. Second, Jesus knew if he was going to meet the demands of the crowd he needed re-enforcement. Here he reveals to us the power of prayer. If he was going to meet the demands of others successfully, he first had to meet with the Father. If he was going to speak meaningfully with the masses, he had to first allow the Father to speak to him. Prayer will never do the task for us. It will, however, strengthen us for the task to be done.

Jesus discovered that only by turning to God when the crowds were pressing so hard against him could he ever hope to maintain a sharp focus on his true reason for being. We need to know when to walk away, when to shut the door, and when to be alone to re-group our thoughts and to re-think God's will and purpose for our lives. If we do not take this time, we could possibly crack under the load, go off in the wrong direction, say the wrong words, or do the wrong things. It is possible that the stress and strain could cause us to go in an opposite direction of our purpose. Suddenly we discover that life is counter-productive from our intentions. In the movie *Bridge Over the River Kwai* the British officer is so busy and so consumed by the bridge he builds that he forgets his responsibilities as an officer, the battle he is fighting, and the human lives for which he is responsible. The purpose of his life at that moment is to lead his men and not to defend his bridge. How easily we can develop a fortress mentality regarding our church and forget the human needs that exist on our doorsteps!

Are We Busy Doing The Wrong Things?

In our busyness are we the church that God intends for us to be? Are we busy doing the right things? What is the right thing? Our task is to hear, proclaim, teach, and spread the good news of God's love for all people in Jesus Christ. We do many things through support groups, self-help programs, recreation of all kinds, sports teams, and social and mission outreach. Every one of them is related to the gospel in some way or another. We must not forget in all of our activity that our purpose is to proclaim the Word and administer the sacraments. No other institution in the world has this responsibility. The church is a social institution like all institutions. As such it has power — institutional power and authority. But the source of the church's power is not the result of being an institution. It is the result of being called by God to proclaim God's Word. When God's Word, the enacted Word (sacrament), the written Word (scripture), the proclaimed Word (Jesus Christ), is properly presented through the Holy Spirit, then the church has power. We need to be faithful to the Word.

Our Responsibility To God's Word

Christians are responsible to declare the Word. Like many of you, I was filled with empathetic pain as I watched *Schindler's List*. Krakow, Poland, had a history for centuries as a stronghold of the Christian faith. One has to ask, "Where was the church?" when all of this was taking place. For fifty years historians have been asking the same question. It is yet to be answered. The church was present, but silent. For over 150 years there was slavery in our land. Where was the church? For the most part, it was silent. Prominent church members were slave holders. The church was so embroiled in the practice of slavery that it became divided into the Northern and the Southern church. What about the Word today? Where is the Word being proclaimed in regard to violence, war, and those deep social issues such as abortion, human sexuality, and race? Where have all the prophets gone?

> *Every morning when the sun comes up, a gazelle wakes. He knows that he must outrun the fastest lion or he will be eaten. When the sun comes up, the lion wakes. He knows that he must outrun the the slowest gazelle, or he will starve. In the end it doesn't matter whether you are a lion or gazelle; when the sun comes up, you better be running.*[1]

How true. We run from sunup to sundown. Chasing and being chased by responsibilities and expectations. Little is left after we deal with all of the demands of the workplace. The little that is left is gobbled up by community and family activities. But, often times, even when the sun goes down, the race still goes on. This morning we come to the table of the Lord. The pace is slowed. It is a moment of withdrawal. A time to catch your breath. A moment to reflect upon the bread, the body of Christ, and the cup, the blood of Christ. God's love for us at this moment has became so visible, so personal, so close, and so reassuring. It is here in these elements of humble access that God through Christ again offers himself to us.

---

1. *Lectionary Homiletics,* Vol. 4, Number 4, March 1993, p. 17.

Mark 1:40-45

Epiphany 6
Ordinary Time 6

A Hands-on Religion

Moved with pity, Jesus stretched out his hand and touched him.

— Mark 1:41

A leper confronted Jesus and said to him, "If you want to, you can make me clean." I would imagine that the crowd around Jesus fell silent. They all gazed at him and wanted to see what he was going to do. They probably said to themselves, "One thing he would never do is touch him." Then they remembered that in his previous healing incidents he did touch those who were sick. "Would he now risk such a thing?" they murmured one to another. What made this such an electrifying moment was the fact that they never knew what Jesus was going to do.

Taking A Risk

We probably have never considered this, but the leper was also taking a risk. Under the law he was not supposed to be within the camp (Leviticus 13:46). He would wear his bell to warn others that he was in the area and they should keep clear. He was among the untouchables, the lowest level on the social ladder. By being where he was, he was risking stern rebuke on the part of the bystanders. They could take violent action against him because they feared the disease so greatly. He also risked disappointment. In the first century, leprosy was a persistent and incurable skin disease. The person was unsightly because of his rotting flesh, and the stench associated with it was unbearable. Once you had it, you had it for a lifetime. There was no getting rid of it. No wonder this man sought out Jesus regardless of the cost and the disappointment. Here was his only hope of being healed of this dreaded disease and being restored to health and society.

In his pleading for cleansing and restoration he was taking a major risk. He may not be healed. He may be rejected. He may be forced by the crowd to go back to his leper colony. Everyone could readily see if his skin was cleansed or not. He couldn't fake it. He was willing to risk all of this and threw himself on the mercy of Jesus. His faith is expressed in his words, "If you choose, you can make me clean." This underscores his firm faith in Jesus. He was convinced that Jesus could restore him physically, spiritually, and socially.

The Response To Human Need

Jesus also ran serious risks in this encounter. His response to the leper's request was first to stretch out his hand and touch him. Then Jesus said to him, "I do choose. Be made clean." A shudder of horror, of revulsion, of consternation and of surprise swept through the crowd. Jesus was always getting himself in trouble in his love and concern for others. He knew what he was doing was risky, but he never gave it a second thought because he was so preoccupied by the cry of human need. Human need took precedence over everything else. No strict Jew would ever venture near anyone who suffered from such a recognizable stigmata. No one in his right senses would risk health and ritual integrity by actually daring to touch the flesh of one who was regarded as so unclean and defiled as this leper. But Jesus did! Without any hesitation he defied priestly and Talmudic ban on approaching and touching an unclean object. This was an anti-traditionalistic and anti-establishment action on his part. Jesus wanted everyone in earshot to hear his direct response to a direct appeal. "I do choose! Be made clean!" Concern for human need that day overrode any desire to maintain legalistic concerns. Jesus was motivated by a deep feeling of compassion and pity for the leper. He gave no thought for his own safety and well-being.

The Incurable Is Cured

Look what happened that day in Galilee. A person who was suffering from the cruel banning from society and was made untouchable had been touched by the healing hands of Jesus. The unapproachable had been approached. The untouchable had been touched. The incurable had been cured. The unclean and the contaminated had been miraculously destroyed and dispersed. And in the words of S.G. Browne, "In that action, a whole world of misjudgments, misunderstandings and mistranslations was swept away."

The important words for us today are Jesus' words "I will." When Jesus was faced with the most dreaded disease in the first century, his intentions were to bring healing. For every sufferer today the main point lies in Jesus' response, "I will." By this reply Jesus shows us that he can in fact heal even the most dreaded diseases, such as leprosy, cancer or AIDS. These words "I will" are words of grace and hope to the leper, but also good news to the reader: God wills healing. God is on the side of the healers.

Going Beyond Stereotypes

This is how Jesus always met men and women. He met them on the level of their need, regardless of who they were or what they had done. He met everyone as human beings, never as stereotypes. Stereotypes were as powerful then as they are now. Once a label is placed on a person the human being vanishes. Many labels were given to people in the New Testament — such labels as tax collector, Samaritan, Roman soldier, prostitute, rich young man, Pharisee, sinner or publican. They all appear in the gospel narrative, and every time Jesus completely ignores the label and deals with the person. This is certainly true of his encounters with Matthew, Zacchaeus, the traveler on the Jericho road, the centurion, Mary Magdalene, and Nicodemus. David H.C. Read points out that "Jesus knew the ugly side of society — the brutality of the occupation, the corruption of the tax system, the racial prejudices, the economic injustice, the religious hypocrisy, and the sexual degradation. But never once did these factors blind him to the reality of the human being, the unique son or daughter of God he saw before him."

From Words To Action

When Jesus was confronted with human need, cautiousness and prudence were not his characteristic traits but compassion, concern and action were. For Jesus religion was a hands-on affair. This is where we as the church run into problems. We have a chronic problem of being able to get things done. We are afflicted in our outreach. Our minds approve the gospel, our hearts have emotionally sincere feelings for love and service, but our concern to help seems to have difficulty getting from our hearts through our minds to our hands. We have difficulty getting our hands and hearts to cooperate. We have been caught up in a "cult of verbal Christianity." We are possessed by the delusion of glowing words. The feeling of many is that if we have talked about something, approved a motion, appointed a committee, or written a definitive paper on the subject then we have done our job. How many church people pass a resolution on racism but never encounter those of another race? How many people take part in heated discussion about how to minister to the homeless, but do not know one homeless person. Jesus in his hands-on approach did the unthinkable thing — he reached out and touched the unclean.

Where Is Christ?

In his book, *Faith Seeking Understanding*, Daniel Migliore points out that since the New Testament it has been the principle of ecclesiology that where Christ is, there is the church. But where is Christ? Christian doctrine would say: Christ is where the bishop is; Christ is where the gifts of the Spirit are manifest; Christ is where the sacraments are celebrated and the Word rightly proclaimed. There is an element of truth in all of these answers, yet none of them explicitly includes the response given in Matthew 25:31ff. It is here that we discover Christ is among the poor, the hungry, the sick, and the imprisoned. Those who minister to the wretched of the earth minister to Christ. Migliore goes on to point out that the true church is not only the church of the *ear* where the gospel is rightly preached and heard. The church is not only the church of the *eye* where the sacraments are enacted for the faithful to see and experience. But the church is also the church of the outstretched helping *hand*. This passage in Matthew 25 reveals clearly to us that Christ is among the poor, and the church is the people of God free enough to enter into solidarity with the poor. Here in Galilee Jesus' encounter with the leper certainly affirms this fact. Today we need to let the church be the church, the body of Christ in the midst of the world. We need to carry on the hands-on ministry that Jesus inaugurated.

I wonder what God thinks about us. Sunday after Sunday we experience the challenge of the gospel in our worship services. We are inspired by God's word and uplifted by the magnitude and splendor of our church music. But after our mountaintop experience together, we allow our hands to fall idle and fail to extend the love of God to others in concrete terms.

I heard a story about a statue of Christ in a church in Europe that was hit by a bomb during World War II. They dug up the statue and discovered that it was undamaged except for the hands that had been broken off. They hired a sculptor to replace the hands. Finally, they decided to leave it like it was as a reminder to the people that Christ has no hands but ours to do his work.

"Jesus stretched out his hands and touched him."

Mark 2:1-12   Epiphany 7
                                    Ordinary Time 7

The Power Of A Rumor

... it was reported that he was at home. So many gathered around that there was no longer room for them, not even in front of the door.
— Mark 2:1-12

Most sermons on this text deal with one of two things: either a detailed account about the four men who carried their paralytic friend to Jesus and, because of the crowd, were forced to open up the roof and lower him into the healing presence of Jesus, or the relationship between forgiveness and healing. But I want to focus our attention on that Capernaum crowd.

It was a warm autumn morning in September and I was driving from Atlanta to Warm Springs, Georgia. I was traveling south on state road 18. The road was desolate. I had it all to myself, occasionally passing a farm or two. I had gone through several small towns that were no more than mere crossroads. Suddenly, I came upon a truck stop and people and cars were everywhere. It was obvious that something was happening and my first thought was that a serious accident had occurred. As I arrived on the scene I noticed two large tractor-trailers and the signs on the side read, "United Artists." As I got closer I saw cameras and technicians, and I knew it was a movie set. Then my wife exclaimed, "There is

Kenny Rogers!" Sure enough, there he was with his silver-gray hair, plaid shirt and blue jeans, standing in the middle of the set. I pulled my car over to the side of the road and joined the crowd.

The crowd that gathered around the set came just as they were. Farmers were dressed in their work clothes and housewives were holding small children. Some of them still had pink curlers in their hair. I thought to myself that somehow the word was out. All of this was the result of the power of a rumor that had traveled rapidly through this rural community. The word spread quickly. The phone lines were burning up with the news that "Kenny Rogers was down at the truck stop on state road 18," and the people came.

The Rumor Spread

Jesus' arrival in Capernaum caused a great deal of excitement. The crowds came and gathered around the house where he was staying. There was no longer any room for people to stand even about the door or the windows. The word had gotten around that Jesus of Nazareth was in town. The rumor spread and the crowds came. This crowd was different than the crowd that came to the truck stop in that rural Georgia town. That crowd came only to see. They wanted to be able to tell their neighbors and friends that they had seen Kenny Rogers, the country singing star.

The crowd in Capernaum came to get something. When the rumor spread that Jesus of Nazareth was in the village, the people wanted to come because he was rumored to be a charismatic teacher and healer. He had a reputation of caring for poor people, especially the deprived, sick, and rejected, so the people came.

Those who came and crowded around the house where Jesus was came for two reasons. First, they came for his teaching. You notice that the text carefully states: "He was teaching the word to them." The people listened because he was not like the scribes and the Pharisees, but he taught as one who had authority. His message was earthy, human, timely, and relevant. He used images, symbols, stories, and parables they could understand. They came to hear what he had to say.

Others came to be healed. An illness, which today we would consider minor and incidental, was life-threatening in the first century and there was little hope of a cure. When a person came upon the scene with a reputation of being a healer, the sick came from all directions with the hope that in some way they would be able to draw upon his healing power. For that reason the crowd that came to Jesus was great and pressed in upon him.

A Generous Person Draws A Crowd

A generous person will always draw a crowd. A person who is generous with his or her time, energy, or skill and who is sincerely interested in people and reveals a sense of care and concern will always find people on his doorstep. Such people know the meaning of the words, "and many people came."

Our church mission team that went to work in the village of Las Tablitos in the Dominican Republic last summer knew what it was "to have the people come." We came among these people to give of ourselves, our time, and our energy. We worked together as Dominicans and Americans. Our team gave of themselves generously to the people and the people sensed it. Together we dug ditches with pick and shovel, mixed concrete, shoveled sand, laid blocks, and painted walls in our effort to erect a new school building in the village. We laughed, worked, sang, ate, and lived together. When we left, we left all of our belongings, except for what we were wearing.

For the two weeks that we were there, the people realized that we were concerned about them and their welfare and so they came, especially for our last night. We wanted to have a time together with the people, so we invited them to come on our last evening to a service that would be held in the building that we had just completed. It was just like the house in Capernaum; they crowded into the small building, filling it to overflowing with men, women, and children from the village. Together we sang, prayed, and shared food as well as the Eucharist. It was a time of celebration. It was an experience that our team members would never forget.

A Loving And Caring Church Draws A Crowd

A loving, caring people always draw a crowd. It is also true that a loving and caring church will always draw a crowd as well.

If a church is not drawing a crowd, it needs to take a careful look at itself. It could be that it is not portraying the loving concern of Christ for the people. It could be that it is not offering anything that is making a difference in people's lives. Our prayer for our church is that we will always be a caring church, with compassion and concern for the needs of others. We pray that what we do here is essential to those who come and that it makes a difference.

Count it all joy when you fall into the problems of others with their needs and requests for help. It means that you have appeared as a caring person. For that very reason, others seek out your counsel and opinion. You may feel that you are being "rushed to death" when in fact you are being "rushed to life."

Erroneously, the easy life has been characterized as one where you are never interrupted; you encounter no jostling crowds, no demands. If you land a job that requires little effort, you may be tempted to feel like you "have it made." A job that is not demanding, requiring little effort on your part, may be the worst thing that could happen to you. It would certainly be a detriment to your creativity and self-fulfillment. Wouldn't you hate to be the Maytag repairman where no one would ever need you? What a bore!

People who like people draw a crowd. Jesus had compassion for the crowds. They came. A church that loves people will always draw a crowd. That's because "people who love people are the happiest people in the world."

Mark 2:13-22　　　　　　　　　　Epiphany 8
　　　　　　　　　　　　　　　Ordinary Time 8

What Shall We Do With The New Wine?

. . . but one puts new wine into fresh wineskins.
— Mark 2:22

Jesus knew that his message was different. In a sense it was startlingly new. He knew that his life was drastically different from that of the orthodox rabbinic teacher. He also knew that it was difficult for his hearers to entertain such new truth. Therefore, he gave them a vivid illustration to show them how important it was to have an open and adventurous mind.

Jesus tells the story about the wine and the wineskins. In those days the wine was stored in animal skins. Since new wine gave off gases and expanded, it was placed in new wineskins, because they were supple, soft, elastic, and capable of expanding with the pressure. Jesus said it would never be advisable to put the new wine into old wineskins, because they were dry and brittle, and had no elasticity. Since they could not expand with the pressure, they would eventually crack open and the wine would be lost.

A Willingness To Accept New Ideas

What does this mean in contemporary terms? Our minds must be elastic enough to receive and contain new ideas. It seems that we must always struggle against the prejudice of a closed mind.

Jesus is well aware that he came with new ideas for a new way of life, containing new concepts of truth. The power of his teachings had the radicalness of a new birth. It was like being born all over again. Because of the resistance of the religious leaders of his day, Jesus knew he was going to have a difficult time. So he shared with his audience this simple parable because he knew of their temptation to keep the old ways of thinking and doing.

The problem with the old skins was their rigidity and inflexibility. Why were these religious leaders so rigid? They sought to defend the faith of their fathers and they did not want an itinerant preacher fooling around with it. They felt it was their calling to defend the integrity of doctrine and belief. This was a very worthy cause in their minds, even if it was at the expense of possible new truth. They had closed minds in regard to new ideas and thoughts, especially about God and God's dealings with men and women. It is similar to a sign I saw in an office which read: "My mind is made up, do not confuse me with the facts."

A Resistance To New Things

At some point in time old ways, manners, words, phrases, creeds, and theology seem to come apart and crack. They grow brittle with time. Like old wineskins they lose their elasticity. Why is there such resistance toward new ideas and possible new life in Christ? One reason may be that such truth would require a change in behavior. The old becomes familiar and comfortable, but the new brings new demands and the possibility of sacrifice. This creates an uneasiness and behavior is not easily changed without a struggle. This newness is expressed clearly by the apostle in 2 Corinthians 5:17: "If anyone is in Christ, there is a new creation, everything old is passed away, see, everything has become new."

Copernicus, who lived in the sixteenth century, was a great astronomer and scientist as well as a Christian. To many church leaders of his day he was a radical because he made a radical new discovery. His *Book of Revolutions* shook the world because in it he introduced his new discovery that the earth is not the center of the universe, rather the sun is and the earth revolves around the sun.

Facing New Discoveries

The Catholic Church demanded he retract his statement. They placed his book on the Index, meaning it was forbidden to be read by Catholics. Catholic Church leaders charged that Copernicus was "a fool who wishes to reverse the entire scheme of astronomy as taught in sacred scripture." The Protestant reformers were just as rigid. Martin Luther declared, "This upstart astrologer deceives the people and reverses the teachings of the Bible. Sacred scripture tells us that Joshua made the sun stand still not the earth." John Calvin answered Copernicus by stating Psalm 93, "God has established the world, it shall never be moved." Copernicus was so discouraged that he decided to withhold his discovery from publication because he loved the church and he did not want to cause any dissension. But he was right. His discovery was truthful. It was a monumental discovery that would greatly benefit the world of astrology and science. Why should such a colossal discovery of truth be withheld because the church could not face the truth of new discovery? His book appeared at last, and one of the first copies reached Copernicus on May 24, 1543. He was on his deathbed at the time. He read the title page, smiled, and in the same hour died.

The parable teaches us that the value is not in the wineskin, but in the wine. There is the tendency to confuse the wineskin with the new wine. When the church became an institution rather than a movement (this happened at the time of Constantine in the fourth century with his Edict of Toleration), it confused the message with the institution. Many turned their attention to protesting the interest of the institution rather than the proclamation of the good news. For many Christians the institution became primary and the message of the gospel became secondary. Christians confused the treasure with the institution that merely housed the treasure. The fact is that the gospel that can radically change human life can be a threat to the survival of the church as an institution. This tension and struggle continue. That is why the wine must always be placed in new winesskins that will have the elasticity and flexibility needed.

Hard to Give Up Old Ways

Each generation must pour the new wine from one perishable vessel to another while preserving the wine (the message) and the old wineskins must be discarded. The message of God's love in Christ remains the same while the forms and structures that communicate that message are ever changing. If not, Christianity becomes merely a creed, a polity, a form, instead of spirit and new life in Christ. It is a pity that we would hold to old forms, allowing the wine of new truth to be spilt.

It is hard for us to give up the old wineskins. We pour the activities of modern Christians into old forms of behavior that were never meant for them. We pour the truth of Christ's teachings into worn out and archaic words and language that no one understands. We pour our newfound joy in Christ into old, formal, stuffy, expressionless forms of worship that excite no one. The new wine of the gospel of good news should not be poured into the legalism of the past.

The city of Miami has gone through tremendous change in the last thirty years, more than any other city in the eastern United States. The churches in Miami have had a difficult time coping with the cultural and racial changes. Prior to the changes, there were three outstanding Methodist churches in Miami that had large memberships and programs. But these three churches had a difficult time facing change. They could not accommodate themselves to the changes that surrounded them. Today those churches are no longer there. They do not exist. A high-rise, a condominium, and a college office building now stand where these three churches once stood. There are other Methodist churches in Miami that did change, becoming culturally diverse, and they have become exciting, growing congregations. Rigidity and resistance result in the loss of opportunity, because the old wineskins break and the new wine is lost.

The Gospel Brings New Truth

Jesus proclaimed a new relationship with God. As one studies the biblical narrative, one discovers that the word of God in Christ brings in a new day, a new order, and a new kingdom. It brings new words: grace and love. It brings in a new direction: "love your enemy and pray for those who misuse you." It brings a new community: they will know you are my disciples, because you love one another. It brings new hope: "Behold, I make all things new."

The defenders of the *status quo,* who felt it was their primary task to defend the faith of their followers against this stranger from Galilee, questioned Jesus, "Why don't you fast like the Pharisees and the disciples of John? Why do you eat with sinners and associate with outcasts? Why do you break the Sabbath law by harvesting, working, and healing on the Sabbath day? By what right do you break such traditions?"

Jesus answered them with a simple parable: No one puts new wine into old wineskins. Because the old skins burst and the new wine is lost. The new wine is put into fresh wineskins.

The question for us is: What are we going to do with the new wine?

Mark 9:2-9   Transfiguration Of The Lord
(Last Sunday After The Epiphany)

With Our Heads In The Clouds

Then a cloud overshadowed them ... .
— Mark 9:7

The crowds were gone. Jesus was alone with his disciples. They sat around the campfire enjoying its warmth as the evening lengthened. They were gazing at the fire in silence, occasionally poking a stick at the logs in order to turn them over, causing the flames to shoot up. Jesus broke the silence: "What are people saying about me?" The disciples looked at one another, waiting for someone to answer. Peter spoke up, "What do you mean?" "Who do the people say that I am?" replied Jesus. They answered, "John the Baptist," "Elijah," "One of the prophets from the dead." After a brief silence Jesus asked, "Who do you say that I am?" Peter answered, "You are Christ, the Messiah of God." They all stared again at the fire. Finally, Jesus broke the silence again, "The Son of Man must suffer many things, and be rejected by the elders and chief priests and scribes, and be killed, and on the third day be raised." No one said a word. The disciples looked at one another with puzzlement and wonder. They were not sure what it all meant.

How strange this sounded to them. It was like having a political candidate tell his followers that in order to win he would have to be defeated in the upcoming election. It did not make sense to them. They were confused. Peter took Jesus aside and said to him, "God forbid, Lord! This shall never happen to you" (Matthew 16:22). He was saying, "Lord, tell us that this is not true." This is not what Peter had in mind when he called Jesus the "Messiah."

The Need To Withdraw

A week later, Jesus took Peter, James, and John and they went up a high mountain to be alone. Jesus felt the need to withdraw. We need that opportunity to withdraw from the clutter and ambiguity of day to day existence. We know that special moment when we can get in touch with the deeper realities of who we are and who God is. We need that mountaintop experience where there is the parting of the veil which hides the infinite from our normal vision. It is that special moment when we can reconfigure the past, envision the future, and empower the present. There are several biblical examples for this. Moses had that mystical experience in the wilderness before the burning bush. It was here that he heard the voice of God. It was only a temporary sojourn. God ordered him back to Egypt to confront an unrelenting dictator to free the slaves. But the wilderness made the Exodus possible. Moses had first to confront God in the wilderness before he could confront Pharaoh in Egypt. In the withdrawal to the wilderness, Moses had his life validated, his task was made clear, and he could then set his face toward Egypt with confidence. What was true for Moses in his wilderness experience was also true for Jesus and Paul. For each of them it was merely an interlude; it lasted for a moment; it was never an end in itself.

But Peter responded as most of us would. He wanted to stay and build three condominiums and settle in rather than go back down to a scary world. But Jesus would have none of it. On the mountaintop the air is thin and the trees are small, short and stubby. There is a beauty, but it is a stark beauty, especially above the timberline where it is mainly rock, dirt and very dry. For growth one has to go to the valley where there is an abundance of rain which produces lush greenery and the richness of color. We visit mountains but we live in the valleys.

This trip to the mountain was not a picnic in the country, but a time to thrash out among themselves an understanding of God's will and purpose. Some great things were about to happen. While Jesus was praying, his appearance changed and his countenance became dazzling white. Suddenly, Moses and Elijah appeared and they were talking to him about his departure and the destiny he was about to fulfill in Jerusalem. But the disciples had fallen asleep. They missed the whole affair.

Prayer Brings Assurance And Direction

This story is wrapped in mystery and intrigue. Jesus' appearance becomes radiant. Moses the law giver and Elijah the prophet appeared to be talking with Jesus. In this single moment the mighty acts of God that brought Israel out of slavery, the gift of the Law, and the ethical charisma of the prophets were all collected and transformed in the person and mission of Jesus the Messiah. How appropriate that it should be the gospel lesson for today. We have come to the end of Epiphany and we are on the threshold of Lent with the observance of Ash Wednesday this week, which leads us into the passion of Jesus.

Luke tells us that this experience occurred while Jesus was praying. "And as he was praying, the appearance of his countenance was altered, and his raiment became dazzling white." This is a pattern that Luke discovered early in his writings about Jesus' life — the most significant things happened while Jesus prayed.

How necessary it is for us to pray. There is an assurance and direction that only prayer can bring to our lives. Jesus was not only assured through prayer that he had chosen the right way, but, more importantly, he now saw the place that Jerusalem and the cross played in his life. Prayer helps us to gain an understanding about the meaning of things that may appear to be random and meaningless.

What are some of those things that we wrestle with? They could be the loss of a job, the decision to get married or not, moral and financial factors, or the course of action to follow. If these factors are important enough to worry about, surely they are important enough to pray about. Jesus gained perspective for his life, especially in regard to suffering and the cross in prayer. Prayer can do that for you. For many, prayer is the last resort, when it ought to be the first. If we could only learn to speak to God in prayer, before we speak to others, how different and more meaningful life would be.

Keeping Alert

In Luke's account, Jesus prayed but the disciples slept. They had fallen asleep. With their heads in the clouds, they drifted off into an unconscious state. Remember the story of Rip Van Winkle? He fell asleep one day in a quiet spot on the banks of the Hudson River and he didn't wake up for twenty years. When he went to sleep, the sign above his favorite tavern read: "King George III, King of England." He was a subject of the British crown. When he woke up, King George was replaced by George Washington and he was an American citizen. The tragic part was that he slept through a revolution. While he snored, oblivious to his surroundings, fantastic, earth-shaking events had taken place. This is what happened to the disciples. They were oblivious to all that was taking place. Don't be too critical of the disciples at this point. Many times we have our heads in the clouds, enclosed in our own little world and losing sight of the larger world, and sleep through great events. How many times are we preoccupied with our own self-importance? We become the prisoners of our own little world of trivialities.

We have little concern in caring for the environment because we have lost touch with nature. We find that our lives, for the most part, have little contact with nature, the soil, trees, and animals. We are not really aware of the larger world around us. How long has it been since you felt the soil in your hands, planted a seed, or cared for a plant? I came across these specal words of Matthew Fox:

> *From the first day I planted things in my front and backyard, I feel a kind of "hugging presence" when I go to bed at night, a mystery of embracing and of beauty and of "being loved" by a different species. I feel the same when I water them, a kind of reciprocal relationship.*

We are so far removed from the world of nature that people don't know the names of trees, plants, and birds anymore. They are nameless. When something loses its name, it loses its meaning for us. It could also lose our respect for its place in God's world of creation.

We miss the wonder and glory of nature because we are not fully awake to it. If we were awake and aware, would we not more often lift our thanks to God in prayers of adoration and thanksgiving? Would we not have greater respect for the created order, if we would remember the gracious love of God that has provided all of this for us?

Our World Is Changing

Today our heads are in the clouds and our minds are in a dream world. We are dreaming the American dream that prosperity will solve most of our problems. I grew up in the late '40s and early '50s and we were constantly treated to the marvels of the time. At school we were vaccinated against polio, ending the fear of what was a dreaded disease. I remember the day the first television set was delivered to our home. I remember when the corner store was replaced by the supermarket overflowing with variety and abundance. I remember seeing for the first time the vapor trail of the new jet plane and staring at it until it disappeared. There was an endless array of gadgets and machines. No problems in those days seemed beyond solution. Good times and American technology seemed to go hand in hand. We were convinced that prosperity was invincible and the Great Society was inevitable. On these two pillars of faith we rested our national identity and our hopes for the future. In those days of the '50s optimism reigned, our churches were full, and we equated middle class values with the Christian life.

Robert J. Samuelson, in a recent article in *Newsweek,* pointed out that every age has its illusions. Ours has been this fervent belief in the power of prosperity. But he reminds us that our pillars of faith are crashing around us. We are painfully discovering that prosperity will not solve all of our personal and social problems. Samuelson states that our good society has been disfigured by poverty, homelessness, racial tensions, the breakdown of the family, uncontrollable crime, staggering budget deficits, and joblessness. The result is a deep crisis of spirit causing self-doubts, cynicism, and confusion as the American dream unravels. He is convinced that we are learning the hard way that prosperity does not automatically provide personal happiness or bring social peace. I would agree that such a dream has become a nightmare.

"And when the disciples awoke they saw his glory" (Luke 9:32). They came back to the world of reality. They were awake and conscious. They came up the mountain with heavy hearts burdened down with Jesus' words about death and a cross. They had questions that were unanswered. Jesus had been talking to them about suffering, rejection, and death. They were not sure what direction their lives were taking, let alone Jesus. Then they woke to the "glory of God." What does the glory of God mean? It means that they were now aware of God's splendor, grandeur, and magnificence. Things were now in a different light. When we awaken to the glory of God, then our homes, our relationships, and our lives become transfigured and radiant. They would leave the mountaintop with many of their questions unanswered. The most difficult moments of their lives were still ahead of them. This, for the most part, is our story. The disciples did not know where all of this was going to lead them. Peter confessed to Jesus, "Lord, it is good for us to be here." This is our confession. "Lord, it is good for us to be here." It is here in this time of worship that we have sensed the "glory of God." The disciples did not know where they were going, but they knew who was going with them. That makes a difference!

Books In This Cycle B Series

Gospel Set

God's Downward Mobility
Sermons For Advent, Christmas And Epiphany
John A. Stroman

Which Way To Jesus?
Sermons For Lent And Easter
Harry N. Huxhold

Water Won't Quench The Fire
Sermons For Pentecost (First Third)
William G. Carter

Fringe, Front And Center
Sermons For Pentecost (Middle Third)
George W. Hoyer

No Box Seats In The Kingdom
Sermons For Pentecost (Last Third)
William G. Carter

First Lesson Set

Light In The Land Of Shadows
Sermons For Advent, Christmas And Epiphany
Harold C. Warlick, Jr.

Times Of Refreshing
Sermons For Lent and Easter
E. Carver McGriff

Lyrics For The Centuries
Sermons For Pentecost (First Third)
Arthur H. Kolsti

No Particular Place To Go
Sermons For Pentecost (Middle Third)
Timothy J. Smith

When Trouble Comes!
Sermons For Pentecost (Last Third)
Zan W. Holmes, Jr.

www.ingramcontent.com/pod-product-compliance
Lightning Source LLC
Chambersburg PA
CBHW071723040426
42446CB00011B/2188